Black Millennials

Black Millennials

Identity, Ambition, and Activism

Edited by Jacquelin Darby

LEXINGTON BOOKS
Lanham • Boulder • New York • London

Published by Lexington Books
An imprint of The Rowman & Littlefield Publishing Group, Inc.
4501 Forbes Boulevard, Suite 200, Lanham, Maryland 20706
www.rowman.com

6 Tinworth Street, London SE11 5AL, United Kingdom

British Library Cataloguing in Publication Information Available

Library of Congress Cataloging-in-Publication Data
Library of Congress Control Number: 2020946697
ISBN 978-1-7936-1181-9 (cloth)
ISBN 978-1-7936-1183-3 (pbk)
ISBN 978-1-7936-1182-6 (electronic)

Table of Contents

Introduction

As a practicing psychologist, I always try to stay up to date with the newest research regarding the populations that I serve. Recently, I have noticed an increase in scholarly articles that are attempting to understand millennials. These articles have touched on several topics about the millennial experience, but not many have taken into account the intersectionality of race. When viewing the available literature, there appears to be a gap where Black Millennials are not given the same academic courtesy that are afforded other cultural groups. This is not to mean that other groups should have less space, rather, it is to say that Black Millennials need to take up more space.

As a practicing psychologist, I am left to speculate on how theories and trends can apply to this unique population that I see daily. As a consumer of research, I question if the incoming news articles, books, and new stories will speak to my unique experience or whether my identities be a footnote in the "future studies" column. As a Black Millennial, I am often left to my own devices when answering the big questions as it relates to my identity.

I decided to create this book with Black Millennials in mind. I wanted this to be a place for individuals to reflect on how certain aspects of millennial life intersect with Black racial identity. This project's aim is to start the conversation by having those who identify as Black Millennials being at the forefront of the discussion. These authors are not only speaking from the academic aspect but are speaking from life experiences. The point of this project is to be a place where their voices are not just a footnote in the conversation but rather are the main viewpoint. This project is to be a place where they are taking up space in a hope to inspire other Black Millennials to speak their truths.

Black Millennials are not a monolith, and the authors do not try to speak for every Black Millennials. They are speaking just for themselves in hopes

1

that others would add their voice to the conversation. It is the hope of this project that it helps other Black Millennials to learn more about themselves and understand how their different identities impact their relationships, their ambitions, and lastly how they impact their involvement in social justice.

Chapter One

The Status of Multiracial Millennials in the Black Community

Marisa G. Franco

According to the U.S. Census (2010), 7.4 percent of people of African descent identify as Multiracial. In 2000, only 4.8 percent of people of African descent identified as Multiracial, demonstrating a 54 percent increase in the number of people of African descent identifying as Multiracial in the last decade (U.S. Census Bureau, 2000). Millennial generations are far more likely to identify as Multiracial than generations past, given that they were among the first generation able to identify with multiple races; the U.S. Census implemented a "check all that apply" approach to census racial categories in 2000 (U.S Census Bureau, 2000). With the number of African-descended Multiracial people forecasted to continue to grow, research must begin to address the positionality of this group within the Black community. Mainly, are they still accepted as members of the Black community, and do they view themselves as members of the Black community? The current chapter examines research on these topics.

I specifically focus on views of and experiences among Black/White Multiracial people throughout this chapter. I do so for two reasons: (1) the Black/White Multiracial community comprises the largest proportion of Multiracial people of African descent in the United States (59.3%; U.S. Census, 2010), and (2) most of the research literature addressing relations between Black and Multiracial people focuses on Black/White Multiracial people. Thus, for the purposes of this chapter, the terms "Multiracial" and "Biracial" are used interchangeably to refer to people of mixed Black and White racial heritage.

In this chapter, I begin by reviewing Black people's perceptions of Black/White Biracial people's status in the Black community. Then, I review research addressing Black/White Biracial people's perceptions of their status in the Black community. Whereas no research studies are explicit about discussing unique experiences and perceptions of Black/White Biracial millennials, most of the research reviewed included participant pools with a mean age within the millennial age window (age 23 to 38 as of 2019)[1] and thus applies primarily to millennials. I additionally discuss specific issues regarding perceptions and experiences of Black/White Biracial millennials at the end of the chapter.

DO BLACK PEOPLE ACCEPT MULTIRACIAL PEOPLE AS MEMBERS OF THE BLACK COMMUNITY?

The historical and legally sanctioned one drop rule indicated that one drop of Black blood makes one Black and relegated people of African descent who were of mixed racial heritage to the Black community (Rockquemore, Brunsma, & Delgado, 2009). This rule effectively allowed White slave masters to amass more slaves by raping their Black female slaves and enslaving the offspring (Rockquemore & Brunsma, 2001). Although the one drop rule is no longer an official government dictum, its ramifications echo in racial classification systems today. In a categorization process called hypodescent, Black/White Multiracial people are more likely to be viewed as Black than White by both Black and White perceivers (Ho, Kteily, & Chen, 2017; Ho, Sidanius, Levin, & Banaji, 2011; Peery & Bodenhausen, 2008).

Black people accept Black/White Biracial people as members of the Black community at high rates (Franco & Holmes, 2016). Indeed, when Multiracial activists advocated for multiple race options on the U.S. Census, the NAACP raised dissent, citing that this practice would fragment the political power of the Black community (Rockquemore & Laszloffy, 2003; Rockquemore et al., 2009), as more people who previously identified as Black would identify as Multiracial. Indeed, given that most African Americans have some White ancestry, what would stop most of the Black community from choosing multiple races rather than a singular Black identity, thus limiting resource allotment to Black communities?

Research demonstrates that one reason why Black people see Black/White Biracial people as members of their racial community is because their shared Black heritage gives them a common susceptibility to racial discrimination, which subsequently fosters a sense of "linked fate" or common destiny between Black and Black/White Biracial people. One study found that at the correlational level, Black people's perceptions of discrimination experienced by Biracial people was linked to their likelihood of applying hypodescent through perceptions of linked fate (Ho et al., 2017). In other words, the more that Black people see Biracial people as vulnerable to racial discrimination, the more likely they are to categorize them as Black, because Biracial people's susceptibility to discrimination engenders a sense of linked fate between Black and Black/White Biracial people. Contrastingly, when Black people experienced a manipulation wherein they were made to believe that Black/White Biracial people experienced less discrimination, they reported less linked fate with Black/White Biracial people and were subsequently less likely to categorize them as Black (Ho et al., 2017). This research speaks to the importance of a shared susceptibility to discrimination in leading Black people to see Black/White Biracial people as members of their racial community.

If susceptibility to racial discrimination drives Black people to categorize Black/White Biracial people as part of their racial in-group, then will Black/White Biracial people who identify as White be less likely to be viewed as a racial in-group by Black people—given that such an identity may be indicative of a diminished susceptibility to racial discrimination? One study found that Black people perceived a Multiracial person who identified as White as less of a racial in-group member than one who identified as Biracial or Black. Black people viewed Multiracial people identifying as Black or Biracial as being equally part of their racial in-group (Smith & Wout, 2019). Furthermore, when Black people received negative feedback from a White-identified versus a Black- or Biracial-identified person, they were more likely to attribute the feedback to racial discrimination (Smith & Wout, 2019). Another study examined whether Black people's empathy toward a Black/White Biracial person experiencing racial discrimination would depend on the Biracial person's racial identity. The study found that Black people empathized equally with a Biracial person identifying as Black or Biracial, but less so with one who identified as White (Franco, Albuja, & Smith, 2019). Furthermore, however, the Biracial-identified target indirectly received less empathy from Black people than the Black-identified target because the former was seen as less Black and generated less linked fate than the latter (Franco et al. 2019). In other words, Multiracial people may sometimes receive less Black in-group resources (i.e., empathy) when they identify as Biracial instead of Black if Black people see the former identity as symbolizing less linked fate with Black people or if it leads Black people to view them as less Black (Franco et al., 2019). All in all, this research suggests that Black people's perceptions of Black/White Biracial people as their racial in-group is malleable based on the identity of the Black/White Biracial person, such that those Biracial people identifying as White are most likely to be excluded, and those identifying as Black are (at least indirectly) most likely to be included. However, overall, Biracial people who identify as such experience high rates of acceptance among Black people, at rates that are comparable to those who identify as Black (Smith & Wout, 2019).

There is variability in Black people's acceptance of Biracial people and Biracial identity. Some Black people see it as a social imperative for Biracial people to identify as Black in order to increase resource allocation to Black people (Thorton, 2009). Black nationalists (i.e, those who believe that Black people should control their own destinies without input from other groups) may be most likely to endorse such an imperative (Franco, Holmes, Swafford, Krueger, & Rice, 2019). In one study, Black people who favored integration of the Black community with other racial groups were more likely to accept Black/White Biracial people as members of the Black community and least likely to impose a Black identity onto them, whereas Black people endorsing Black nationalist ideologies were more most likely to reject them and impose a Black identity (Franco, Holmes et al., 2019). Perhaps, Multiracial people's mixed racial heritage represents integration to Black nationalists, which makes them less likely to accept the Black/White Multiracial group as part of the Black community. Furthermore, the study found that the more that Black nationalists experience racial discrimination, the more likely they are to impose a Black identity onto Black/White Multiracial people (Franco, Holmes et al., 2019). The authors interpretation of this finding was that Black nationalists, by definition, aim to address racism by establishing solidarity with Black people (e.g., Sellers et al., 1997), and that as nationalists experience more racism, they may experience more urgency in achieving Black solidarity, and may do so via imposing a Black identity onto Black/White Multiracial people.

Another factor that influences whether Black people see Black/White Biracial people as part of their racial community is Black people's level of egalitarianism, defined as the degree to which they endorse equality—rather than hierarchy—among racial groups. One study found that Black people higher in egalitarianism were more likely to categorize Black/White Multiracial people as Black because they viewed Black/White Multiracial people as experiencing more racial discrimination and subsequently experienced more linked fate with Multiracial people (Ho et al., 2017). This finding may have arisen because Black people higher in egalitarianism are more sensitive to discrimination experienced by Black/White Biracial people, and thus feel closer to them, given a shared experience of and susceptibility to discrimination.

To conclude, generally, Black people see Black/White Multiracial people as members of their racial community. They are more likely to accept Multiracial people identifying as Black or Biracial than those identifying as White. Furthermore, Black people who endorse integration and egalitarianism may be more likely to see Black/White Biracial people as part of their racial ingroup, whereas Black nationalists may be less likely.

DO BLACK/WHITE MULTIRACIAL PEOPLE SEE THEMSELVES AS MEMBERS OF THE BLACK COMMUNITY?

Black/White Multiracial people can identity in a variety of different ways. Some identify as Black, others as White, and others as Biracial. Still, some identify their racial identity as shifting across contexts, and others opt for a "transcendent" identity wherein they do not identify with racial groups at all (Rockquemore & Brunsma, 2001). In one study of racial labeling among approximately 37,000 Multiracial college freshman, 70.7 percent of Black/White Biracial people identified as Biracial, 24.8 percent identified as Black, and 4.5 percent identified as White. If identity can be used as a proxy to represent the group in which one feels belonging, then with the variety in racial identity choices among the Black/White Biracial population, it is important to clarify whether Black/White Biracial people see the Black community as their "racial home" and factors that might affect such a decision. Research addressing this topic is reviewed within this section.

Overall, Black/White Biracial people report belonging more with Black people than White people. A study by Pew Research Center (2015) found that this group is three times more likely to report commonalities with Black people than with White people (58% vs. 19%), and they report being twice as likely to feel accepted among Black people than White people (58% vs. 25%). These findings make sense, given the historical one drop rule, and because of Black/White Biracial people and Monoracial Black people's common susceptibility to racial discrimination from White people. Indeed, the same survey found that Black and Black/White Multiracial people experience similar amounts of racial discrimination (Pew Research Center, 2015).

Still, some Biracial people report a degree of negative treatment from Black people, particularly in regard to Black people invalidating their racial identity. One study found that Black/White Biracial people reported that Black people invalidated their racial identity more so than any other racial group, and also that they were most hurt when their identity was invalidated by Black people, compared to when it was invalidated by other groups (Franco & Franco, 2015). Furthermore, Biracial people whose racial identity was most invalidated by Black people reported higher rates of racial homelessness (e.g., the sense that they have nowhere to belong racially), and also more challenges with their racial identity (Franco & Franco, 2015). Black people may invalidate Black/White Multiracial people's identity because Black/White Biracial people do not conform to Black cultural practices, because their appearance is not racially prototypical, or because of their part-White ancestry (Franco, Katz, & O'Brien, 2016).

When Black/White Biracial people identify less with the Black community, they may do so for a number of reasons. First, more affluent Biracial people are more likely to identify as White and less likely to identify as

Black (Davenport, 2016). Jewish Biracial people are three times more likely to identify as White than Black, and Baptist Biracial people are 56 percent less likely to identify as White than religiously nonaffiliated Biracial people (Davenport, 2016). Black/White Biracial people who have lived among more Black people were less likely to identify as White (Davenport, 2016). Overall, these research findings suggest that Black/White Biracial people's exposure to different racial communities plays a role in their racial identity, such that they may identify with racial groups to which they are more exposed.

Rockquemore and Brunsma (2002) examined factors that exert an influence on Black/White Biracial people's racial identity. They found that when Black/White Biracial people experienced negative treatment from Black people, they were less likely to identify as Black. Familiarity with Black or White racial group pulls Biracial people toward identifying with that group (Rockquemore & Brunsma, 2002). The study also found that people's identity was affected by their conception of how others viewed their skin color, such that Biracial people tended to identify in ways that aligned with their understanding of others' perception of their skin color (Rockquemore & Brunsma, 2002). Thus, it is likely that Biracial people identify in ways that align with how others perceive them, perhaps to avoid the painful experience of having their racial identity invalidated (Franco & O'Brien, 2018).

In sum, research suggests that Black/White Biracial people's racial home is more so among Black people than White people. However, Biracial people are less likely to identify as Black when they have experienced negative treatment from Black people or else when they have been exposed mostly to White people. Furthermore, though Black/White Biracial people report commonality and acceptance from Black people, they also report rejection of their racial identity from Black people. Given that the Black community may comprise Black/White Biracial people's predominant racial home, rejection of Biracial identity from Black people is particularly deleterious to Biracial people's racial identity and sense of belonging.

BLACK AND BLACK/WHITE MULTIRACIAL MILLENNIALS

Millennials are more likely to identify as Multiracial than any age cohort that has come before them (Pew Research Center, 2016). Furthermore, postmillennials are still more likely to identify as Multiracial. The Multiracial group comprises the fastest growing racial group in America (Farley, 2001), and thus, it is likely that the proportion of African-descended people who identify as Multiracial will continue to rise. The millennial generation is distinct from generations past in that within this cohort more people of African descent identify as Multiracial than ever before. Whereas the rise in a Multiracial identity has raised concerns about fragmentation within the Black community (Rockquemore & Laszloffy, 2003), findings reviewed in the current chapter indicate that a Multiracial identity is not antithetical to Black solidarity. Specifically, Multiracial people identity as such and still largely report feeling at home among Black people (Pew Research Center, 2015), and Black people largely accept Multiracial people who identify as such within their racial communities (Franco & Holmes, 2016; Smith & Wout, 2019). Thus, the millennial generation pushes society to consider race with more complexity, wherein belonging amid the Black community is not determined by a singularly Black identity.

REFERENCES

Davenport, L. D. (2016). The role of gender, class, and religion in Biracial Americans' racial labeling decisions. *American Sociological Review, 81,* 57–84. doi: 10.1177/0003122415623286

Farley, R. (2001). *Identifying with multiple races: A social movement that succeeded but failed?* (Population Studies Center Report 01–491). Ann Arbor: University of Michigan.

Franco, M. G., Albuja, A., & Smith, R. (2019). How Black is Biracial? Black people's empathy towards Black/White Biracial people. Manuscript submitted for publication.

Franco, M. G., & Franco, S. A. (2015). Impact of identity invalidation for Black Multiracial people: The importance of race of perpetrator. *Journal of Black Psychology, 42,* 530–548. doi: 10.1177/0095798415604796

Franco, M. G., & Holmes, O. (2016). Biracial group membership scale. *Journal of Black Psychology, 43,* 1–16. doi: 10.1177/0095798416657260

Franco, M. G., Holmes, O. L., Swafford, F., Krueger, N., Rice, K. (2019). An examination of relationships between Black people's racial identity and their acceptance of Multiracial people. *Group Processes and Intergroup Relations.* Advance online publication. doi: 10.1177/1368430218820957

Franco, M. G., Katz, R., & O'Brien, K. M. (2016). Forbidden identities: A qualitative examination of racial identity invalidation for Black/White Biracial individuals. *International Journal of Intercultural Relations, 50,* 96–109. doi: 10.1016/j.ijintrel.2015.12.004

Franco, M. G., & O'Brien, K. M. (2018). Racial identity invalidation with Multiracial individuals: An instrument development study. *Cultural Diversity and Ethnic Minority Psychology, 24,* 112–135. doi: 10.1037/cdp0000170

Ho, A. K., Kteily, N. S., & Chen, J. M. (2017). "You're one of us": Black Americans' use of hypodescent and its association with egalitarianism. *Journal of personality and social psychology, 113*(5), 753–768. doi: 10.1037/pspi0000107

Ho, A. K., Sidanius, J., Levin, D. T., & Banaji, M. R. (2011). Evidence for hypodescent and racial hierarchy in the categorization and perception of biracial individuals. *Journal of Personality and Social Psychology, 100,* 492–506. doi: 10.1037/a0021562

Peery, D., & Bodenhausen, G. V. (2008). Black + White = Black: Hypodescent in reflexive categorization of racially ambiguous faces. *Psychological Science, 19,* 973–977. doi:10.1111/j.1467-9280.2008.02185.x

Pew Research Center. (2015). Multiracial in America: Proud, diverse and growing in numbers. Retrieved from http://www.pewsocialtrends.org/2015/06/11/multiracial-in-america/

Pew Research Center. (2016). Biggest share of Whites in U.S. are boomers, but for minority groups it's millennials or younger. Retrieved July 5, 2019, from https://www.pewresearch.org/fact-tank/2016/07/07/biggest-share-of-whites-in-u-s-are-boomers-but-for-minority-groups-its-millennials-or-younger/

Rockquemore, K. A., & Brunsma, D. L. (2001). *Beyond Black: Biracial identity in America.* Thousand Oaks, CA: Sage.

Rockquemore, K. A., & Brunsma, D. L. (2002). Theories, typologies, and processes of racial identity among Black/White Biracials. *The Sociological Quarterly, 43,* 335–356.

Rockquemore, K. A., Brunsma, D. L., & Delgado, D. J. (2009). Racing to theory or re-theorizing race? Understanding the struggle to build a multiracial identity theory. *Journal of Social Issues, 65,* 13–34. doi:10.1111/j.1540-4560.2008.01585.x

Rockquemore, K. A., & Laszloffy, T. A. (2003). Multiple realities: A relational narrative approach in therapy with Black-White mixed-race clients. *Family Relations: An Interdisciplinary Journal of Applied Family Studies, 52,* 119–128. doi:10.1111/j.1741-3729.2003 .00119.x

Sellers, R. M., Rowley, S. A. J., Chavous, T. M., Shelton, J. N., & Smith, M. A. (1997). Multidimensional inventory of Black identity: A preliminary investigation of reliability and construct validity. *Journal of Personality and Social Psychology,* 805–813.

Smith, R. J., & Wout, D. A. (2019). Blacks' perception of a Biracial's ingroup membership shapes attributions to discrimination following social rejection. *Cultural Diversity and Ethnic Minority Psychology.* Advance online publication. doi: 10.1037/cdp0000267

Thorton, M. C. (2009). Policing the borderlands: White- and Black-American newspaper perceptions of Multiracial heritage and the idea of race, 1996–2006. *Journal of Social Issues, 65,* 105–123. doi: 10.1111/j.1540-4560.2008.01590.x

U.S. Census Bureau. (2000). *The Black population: 2000.* Retrieved July 5, 2019, from https://www.census.gov/prod/2001pubs/c2kbr01-5.pdf

U.S. Census Bureau. (2010). *The two or more races population: 2010.* Retrieved from https://www.census.gov/prod/cen2010/briefs/c2010br-13.pdf

NOTE

1. Exceptions include Ho, Kteily, & Chen (2017), Thorton (2009), and Pew Research Center (2015).

Chapter Two

The Complexity of Color

Observations and Thoughts on Combating Colorism

Neffer-Oduntunde A. Kerr

COMPLEXITY OF COLOR

According to Merriam-Webster, the definition of colorism is prejudice or discrimination against individuals with a dark skin tone, typically among people of the same ethnic or racial group. Although accurate, this definition barely scratches the surface of how problematic and deeply disturbing colorism is. Those few defining words provide no explanation to its origins, its impact, its damage, or the large-scale social, emotional, and psychological duress it has caused countless individuals. Most will acknowledge that the origins of colorism are rooted in racism, colonialism, and the historical need white people have always had to control black and brown people. In 2019, colorism still seems to be a very prevalent issue since its inception.

For the most part, colorism has been perpetuated mainly by individuals within communities it negatively impacts most (our own). Negative beliefs, behaviors, patterns, and ideologies based on skin color have been passed through generations. Now some may argue that colorism is a thing of the past, something from Jim Crow or our grandparents' era, not a problem for millennials. Yet, disputing the existence of colorism translates into negating the very real testimonies and experiences of those directly affected. It's presence is evidenced by the incessant subtle and blatant occurrences experienced ad nauseum in academia, entertainment, various forms of media, advertising, personal and professional spaces, dating, and more. Colorism is alive and well, but in the last decade, there has been a major shift. Many Black Millennials have become tired of the status quo and have started challenging toxic ideologies connected to colorism by raising awareness and

creating content, products, and services that are influencing various industries and forcing change. The question is, how do we, as a collective, break
this generational curse that is colorism? How do we move forward in combating it in our own community this day in age?

SKIN DEEP

Across the world, colorism has roots based in colonialism. To this day, it can
be found plaguing Black and Brown people of all different countries and
cultures, and on every continent where members of a particular group vary in
skin tone. However, in the United States, colorism can directly be attributed
to slavery.

> While dark-skinned slaves toiled outdoors in the fields, their light-skinned
> counterparts usually worked indoors at far less grueling domestic tasks. Slave
> owners were partial to light-skinned slaves because they often were family
> members. Slave owners frequently forced slave women into sexual inter-
> course, and light-skinned offspring were the telltale signs of these sexual
> assaults. While slave owners didn't officially recognize their mixed-race chil-
> dren, they gave them privileges that dark-skinned slaves didn't enjoy. Accord-
> ingly, light skin came to be viewed as an asset in the slave community. (Nittle,
> 2019)

Passing

Due to the incessant rape of masters to slaves, and the children born from
that, as a result, on average, African Americans have up to 24 percent European ancestry. By the end of America's 246 years of slavery (1619–1865),
there was so much generational intermixing, that there were a small minority
of Black slaves who, in all appearance, who looked 100 percent European
(Johnson, 2019). As a result, many of these Black people who appeared to be
White realized that they would be treated better and have a chance at "better"
(worse in other ways) quality of life if they pretended to live their lives as
White people. This is what became known as 'passing,' The benefit of passing in American history was the chance to live a life with the full rights of an
American citizen, social and economic. An escape from the threat of racial
violence in all its forms, from powerlessness and political disenfranchisement. The price, however, was total exile (Johnson, 2019).

One of the more recent, popular, and shocking cases of passing has been
that of Broadway legend Carol Channing. Channing became a Hollywood
actress in the 1940s and had a career that lasted up until her death in 2019.
She lived her life as a White woman, keeping her true identity a secret for 70
years. It was only in 2003 where she shared that she had known since she
was 16 and that she was proud of her Black ancestry but came into Holly-

wood during a time where she may not have been afforded the same opportunities living as a Black woman. The ability to pass oneself off as White—to choose between living with their existing identity or adopt the dominant racial identity—is the most extreme colorism privilege (Johnson, 2019). What is more interesting is that while their White contemporaries were normally oblivious to the true identities of those passing, there are countless stories about how other Black people could always seem to tell when someone among them was passing. However, there was only a small population of Black people who had the phenotypes to successfully pass and live as Whites. So, for colorism to flourish, that meant there would have to be some type of caste system that valued lighter over darker skin so that the Black people (still living as Black) could feel as though they, too, had some type of privilege over other members of their community.

Colorism as a Tool for Classism

Colorism did not disappear after slavery ended in the United States. In Black America, those with light skin received employment opportunities off-limits to darker-skinned Blacks. This is why upper-class families in Black society were largely light-skinned. Soon, light skin and privilege were linked in the Black community (Nittle, 2019). Due to the fact that many of the lighter Black people found themselves being treated somewhat better by White people, a significant amount of them started actually believing they were. They began to only interact and intermingle with one another, while looking down on their darker hued counterparts. They created groups and social clubs with color-based criteria for membership. One of the most heinous being the notorious "brown paper bag test," used by social clubs within the black community to discriminate against any person darker than a literal brown paper bag (Johnson, 2019). This snowballed into a series of collective actions, behaviors, and patterns that created a very poisonous color-based caste system within the Black community that would continue through generations.

A Generational Curse

There are many Black and Brown people who egregiously think "lighter" skin is better. Many of them saw, heard, or experienced situations that reinforced this thinking. And as a result, they too passed those beliefs to others. The problem is that this perpetuates a poisonous and traumatizing ideology to their children and others around them which has very lasting and damaging effects. One of the reasons colorism is so hard to combat is because it is passed down in a multilayered way, very similarly to racism. Thoughts, behaviors, and words are the tools used to promote it, which makes it very hard to fight because it lives in the minds of others.

There are institutional ways it is integrated into society in how individuals are treated socially and professionally, as well as in regard to everyday optics in advertising, entertainment, and the beauty industry. And also, like racism, colorism is passed down generationally. This toxic generational way of thinking and behaving manifested negative sayings and phrases that sadly some still hear to this day. There are countless documented accounts of individuals being told things from others in their community like "make sure you stay out of the sun" (as not to get any darker than they already were). There were even numerous instances of people pressured or encouraged by family and friends to "marry lighter" for the sake of status and potentially lighter offspring. The colorism knife can often cut both ways, and while individuals with more melanin have historically had to deal with way more blatant and subconscious foolishness, it hasn't always been peaches-and-cream for their lighter counterparts either. In those particular instances, sometimes it was a matter of never truly knowing if they were really wanted or simply chosen to "lighten up" or maintain the bloodline of someone taught to marry or breed "up" (as it was sometimes called). All of these types of psychological aggressions, over time based in colorism, predisposed a partic-ular perceived preference for many.

PREFERENCE OR PROGRAMMING

There are some who would argue that having a particular attraction or affin-ity based on complexion is just a matter of preference. However, that can be vigorously challenged considering that Black and Brown people all over the world have been inundated with and held to European standards of beauty for centuries. What if this proclamation of "that's just my preference" isn't really a preference, but actually a predisposition to what people have been predomi-nantly programmed to believe. What if those beliefs, imposed by the popula-tion in control, have influenced everyone and dictate what was considered good, beautiful, and of value (anything close to whiteness). While anything considered evil, bad, or worthless was connected to blackness. This is includ-ing, but not limited to skin color.

Even language and terminology have been strategically used in ways to reinforce colorism. Words and phrases like black magic, black hearted, black balled, black mail, blacklist, black out, all have negative connotations. While words and phrases like white magic, white lies, white knight, and white flag, are reflective of purity, innocence, and goodness. It is also no secret that those in control of the media, entertainment industry, advertisements, and society alike have always somehow made anything darker either "bad" or "inferior" in some way—even if done in a highly passive or subtle manner. There are a plethora of old TV shows, publications, cartoons, and movies predominantly showing White or lighter individuals as the heroes, beauties, or protagonists. While villains, antagonists, and characters considered undesirable were regularly portrayed as darker. Imagine how a lifetime of this nonstop can consciously and subconsciously affect people. One could easily propose that it leaves one group internalizing ideals of superiority, and another of inferiority, even if they are not aware of it. In turn, it can have a significant effect on preferences. If the tables were turned, and everything was in reverse, the preferences that a lot of people claim to have might be the exact opposite.

There really are not too many topics that are not uncomfortable to address in conversations around colorism. Attempting to discern preference versus programming will always be an ongoing debate. The question can always be asked if an individual has personal preferences that they have formed on their own (genuine preference), or is it just a predisposition to programming. However, it is important not to assume either, but to instead seek understanding in why people operate the way that they do. What is understood for sure is that various forms of programming that perpetuate colorism have always been prevalent, and Black and Brown people have always been exposed to it. The interesting thing about the black experience, though, is that it is not the same for everyone. We know that one Black person does not represent or speak for all Black people, despite whatever the shared experiences may be. Some may have been heavily influenced by these types of programming, others moderately, while some not at all.

One person's truth is not universal, and while certain experiences are shared on a macrolevel as a collective (i.e., colorism), other experiences (like how it manifests for the individual) may not necessarily be parallel to the next person's experience. This is important to address because while speaking to the mistreatment of those who are more heavily melanated (which is documented and very real), it is not everyone's experience. Just like "all Black people didn't grow up poor and in the ghetto," not all darker hued individuals have experienced ill treatment or grew up in environments where they were made to feel anything negative connected to skin tone. However, a significant amount can attest to mistreatment, disrespect, bullying, and worse, and that is enough to make conscious decisions to change this. The aforementioned issues and more have been contributing factors in regard to why colorism is still alive and well and remains to be a problematic issue for many Black and Brown millennials, but thankfully we are seeing a shift.

THE SHIFT

While there is still a good amount of nonsense and ignorance being pro-moted—like skin bleaching being encouraged and some popular singers having a "no dark skin women" rule allowed in his VIP section—there is also a noticeable shift in how more people are choosing to push aside colorism. As with many things, Black women are leading the charge of changing the expiring narrative of what is and is not considered beautiful. Many people are now rejecting antiquated ideologies based on one dimensional European beauty standards that have been reinforced by colorism. And if it's one thing millennials know how to do well, it is to celebrate themselves. That is no exception when it comes to identifying, highlighting, and promoting Black forms of beauty. Many millennials got tired of waiting to see themselves in certain arenas and platforms, so they created their own and made multiple industries take note, change how they market, and change what they create as well.

Influencers

Social media has changed the landscape of how many things are done in this day and age. From the selling of products, sharing of information, to even engaging in activism, people are influenced more and more by how they receive information through social media. Celebrities and influencers who have a large following are often able to get their ideas and messaging across by using their platform on social media to do so. This has definitely been the case in regard to individuals who have pushed back on cliché societal standards that did not include them and who created their own lanes.

Many Black women who are social media influencers have used their platform as a springboard to combat colorism, championing for women of all shades and hues to be seen. These women are their own muses, sharing themselves with the world while simultaneously creating new standards in the beauty industry. Nyma Tang (@nymatang) is one of them. She is a beauty, fashion, and makeup influencer who has openly spoke about the challenges that deeply melanated women in the world still deal with (despite more representation and the perceived celebration of darker skin online). In addition to Tang, there are others like beauty blogger Karla Tobie (@karlatobie) who have gone a step further and have challenged the current inclusion (or lack thereof) practices of certain companies. Tobie holds them accountable by demanding there be representation of Black women expressed in their branding and marketing if they wish to do business with her. And with the massive worldwide following she has, they definitely want to do business with her. She uses her platform not only for herself, but so that other women feel seen as well. Other celebrities and influencers—like Amanda Seales

(@amandaseales), Jessie Woo (@thejessiewoo), and Amara La Negra (@amaralanegraaln)—have been very vocal as well about how nonsensical and problematic colorism is, how it affects people, and how melanin is a thing of beauty and pride.

Beauty

When Rihanna unveiled her Fenty cosmetic line in 2017, it was groundbreaking. In the past, there have been cosmetic companies that have offered a small array of products that catered to individuals with varying levels of melanin. However, in many cases, those needing powders and foundations of darker hues could rarely find them and oftentimes would have to mix various products together to create something that matched their complexion. What was so special about Fenty cosmetics was that its foundation collection was not only inclusive of nearly every shade found among people of color, but it also provided products that complemented the deepest of skin tones. This was done intentionally, and Rihanna was very clear about wanting to make sure there was adequate representation in her products for customers with deeper skin tones who had been ignored for so long.

Fenty was intentional about challenging colorism globally and put heavily melanated individuals at the forefront of its advertising. In doing so, it changed not only how other companies advertised, but the very products they created. This in itself was radical because no major cosmetic company had ever created such an extensive line of products that was this inclusive of black women. There were also additional companies founded by other black women. The Lip Bar, Ka'oir, The Crayon Case, and Juvia's Place all created products specifically with Black and Brown customers in mind. Many of these products are more highly pigmented so that they would complement darker skin tones better, whereas products made by other companies in the past neglected details like that.

Due to the pressure of keeping up with a changing beauty industry, more companies have been exposed for their blatant role in ignoring darker hued demographics of men and women. This can be clearly evidenced by the lack of "nude" or "flesh tone" options that were available to for so long. Companies would literally only create one shade that complemented only a certain group of people. For years, it was the universal color for nude and flesh tone undergarments, shoes, bras, and some lingerie. This was despite the fact that there are a myriad of shades that people come in. Even professional performers and dancers of color would have to dye their own tights to match their skin because at a certain point none existed. Thanks to people demanding representation combined with the pressure of black buying power, more companies are now producing products for all skin tones in order to stay sustainable.

Entertainment

We are now starting to see more and more women with darker skin gracing magazine covers, television screens, social media timelines, movie screens, and commercials and more who reflect what was once heavily ignored and rarely put at the center of attention. Actresses like Lupita N'yongo, who is known for her beauty, as well as others like Viola Davis and Danielle Brooks have been very vocal about the negative effects colorism has had on them in their lives and are a part of the ones leading the charge on changing the narrative on beauty.

In 2018, Jamaican dancehall artist/*Love & Hip Hop: Atlanta* cast member Spice (Grace Hamilton) shocked the world by deleting everything on her Instagram account and replacing it with one photo of her with white skin, blonde hair, and blue eyes. This was shocking because the day before she was a beautiful black woman known for being proud of that. What would later be revealed about her actions was that through shock value, she had decided to use her platform and craft to tackle colorism head on. And she knew it had to be drastic for anyone to pay attention, care, or even talk about it.

Her reasoning for doing this was to bring attention to the fact that color-ism is very real, painful, and something she constantly has to deal with in the entertainment industry as well as her home country. Hamilton shared that the infractions range from subtle microaggressions to blatant disrespect in regard to her skin tone as a darker woman. She shared instances of being told how she should change her look to be more appealing (according to European standards of beauty), should maybe consider "brownin" (which is slang for skin bleaching in Jamaica), or flat out being told that yes, she's talented, but if she were lighter she could or would have gotten further in her career.

Hamilton highlighted how she and countless others incessantly deal with colorism from all angles, but it is most hurtful and prevalent within her own community. She coined the phrase "Black Hypocrisy" (which is also the title of her song). Black Hypocrisy calls out the hypocritical behavior among black and brown people toward each other by playing into colorism. The artist even shared that some of the harshest criticism about her skin tone would often come from individuals who were the exact same shade as she was. Spice understands through firsthand experience how damaging and tox-ic colorism is. She is a major proponent and advocate committed to disman-tling it. Through her words and music, and by showing how proudly she loves her own beautiful skin, it is her goal that more will love theirs as well, despite what this cruel world and others have taught them to feel or believe.

Canadian rapper, singer/songwriter Tory Lanez publicly took a stand against colorism while shooting a video on set. The director stopped to replace the darker skin model with one who had light skin. Lanez objected to this and had the previous woman reinstated for the scene. To people who are not cognizant of colorism, especially in the entertainment industry, this may seem insignificant, a simple matter of one model being chosen over the other. However, this was huge to those who understand it and how those in the industry have always treated individuals with darker skin. Lanez doing something as simple as not letting a director replace a darker skin dancer with a lighter one showed two things: (1) that he is very aware of the issues connected to colorism, and (2) that he would not allow that model to be made to feel less than in that instance because of the concentration of her melanin. Lanez later took to social media stating:

> [T]his is an on-going problem in our community of entertainment that needs to stop. As a black man, sometimes I'm going to joke about the black community just like we all do. But what I'm not going to do is allow any of these Directors to de-value our black women. Countless times I've seen directors swap out our women of color for women of lighter complexion, or women with straighter hair, etc. It is our responsibility as artists to stand up and not let this happen. It's BEEN time to embrace our woman of color. #BlackIsBeautiful (Sanders, 2019)

There are other artists intentionally finding ways through their craft to combat colorism with songs that have messages that point it out and/or celebrate the beauty of melanin. In the rap song "Complexion" Kendrick Lamar gives his audience historical context and shows that he is well aware of the ugly history of rape in this country that created so many different skin tones among Black people. Through the chorus he reinforces how they are all beautiful and how complexion really doesn't matter. Beyonce's "Brown Skin Girl" from her latest album, "The Lion King: The Gift," had girls and women around the world celebrating their beautiful brown skin in 2019 (Davis, 2019). Through this high level acknowledgment and praise of melanated individuals those with such a huge platform will hopefully encourage better treatment for all not only across the entertainment industry but in the world.

THIS AIN'T EVEN YO' PROBLEM

I didn't grow up in a household where skin tone predicated privilege or beauty. At home, I was never made to think, feel, or believe that I was prettier or better than anyone else because I was of a lighter complexion. In our family, every member was a different skin tone ranging from very light to very dark (and everything in between). My parents taught my siblings and I that Black is beautiful. In fact, my father always talked to us about how beautiful people who were heavily melanated were. There were numerous sculptures, posters, paintings, and books of beautiful black faces and forms throughout our home. A huge poster of Judith Jamison, from the dance company Alvin Ailey, hung in the living room (it is still there to this day). I grew up seeing black women of all shades as beautiful and whether she was light or dark was an unimportant factor, because from childhood, I was taught beautiful is simply beautiful.

Unfortunately, I would eventually learn that that was not how the world worked outside of our home. I stayed having to fight and wipe tears from my younger sister's face when she would get bullied and told she was not as pretty because her skin was darker (she's actually very pretty). There were plenty of times where I was jumped and had to fight other girls harmed by colorism, many of whom were simply hurt or angry because some of them had been treated so harshly about their own skin color. I was a reminder of how they had been made to feel. It didn't take long for me to learn that when it came to skin color, our people had serious challenges. I noticed how they would treat my heavily melanated younger brother differently and how I couldn't go anywhere alone with my mother without people assuming I must have had a white father. I don't.

I share these experiences as a frame of reference. I am very aware and cognizant of the harsh realities connected to colorism. Sadly, there are still many Black and Brown people in our community who egregiously think lighter skin is better and perpetuate a poisonous and traumatizing ideology to their children and others around them which has very lasting and damaging effects. This "thing," colorism, which really isn't even an actual thing, but a mentality, has pitted family members and friends against each other. It has been used as a tool in genocide (Rwanda). It has created such a divisiveness throughout the world and paved the way for negative behaviors, emotions, triggers, and traumas which can all be attributed to colorism.

There have been times when I have addressed the issue of colorism and have been asked why does it even matter to me? Why do I even care (with the implication that it's not my problem)? However, the truth is, colorism is a tool used to alienate and disenfranchise us all perpetually. This is why everyone should care about colorism within the community even if they do not harbor colorist ideals.

Essentially, it is important for us all to care and do better. So I speak to this issue and wrote this for the people in my life and those I've never met who have been most affected by the toxicity that is colorism. I do it for my niece, Isabella, whose melanin is beautiful and as rich as the earth. Yet, at ten years old she has already experienced color-based cruelties. So until we, as a community, rid ourselves of this cancer called colorism, I will always champion for deeply melanated skin to be celebrated, represented, seen, and branded as beautiful.

COMBATING COLORISM

Colorism feels like a bad "haint" or spirit that's always around, always lingering, waiting for an opening, a conduit, a willing participant to do its dirty work. Sometimes we like to act as if it doesn't exist—that is, until it rears its ugly head in the form of divisiveness through skin tones and hues. Even the guise of joking or playing when it comes to skin tone doesn't take away from the sting of colorism either. And those on the opposite ends of the skin tone spectrum seem to feel it way more than those who fall in the middle. And by "middle" I mean those who fall in the "too light to be dark, and too dark to be light" category. This is one of those things that affects all Black and Brown people whether acknowledged or not. And some deal with the negative effects of it much more than others. While it can be perpetuated by all people (even those it affects in no way), it is most damaging when done to and by those within our own communities. One has to wonder how are we to address the issue of colorism if it is so heavily ingrained.

One of the things we can do first is to start with ourselves on an individual level by retraining and redirecting our thoughts and actions. To an extent, everyone has been exposed to or affected by some kind of manifestation of colorism. This is why self-reflection is key, especially when it comes to having to identify our own individual connection, experiences, and roles in either playing into, being passive, or rejecting colorism. It is important to examine these things because doing so can open the way for combatting it altogether. And because this "affliction" lives in people's minds and is passed to others through thoughts and beliefs, then it is the mind where we must go to fix it.

Changing behaviors is also key. There is nothing wrong with finding someone's skin beautiful and telling them. But it is a very different thing to tell that woman that she is pretty then adding the infamous and insulting "for a dark skin girl." As if her being is pretty is despite her melanin, not as a part of her overall beauty. If you compliment someone, simply compliment them because saying things like that are backhanded compliments, which is really an insult. It is also vital to control what we allow others to say and do to us and those we love, especially our children. Family or not, do not allow others to pass their toxic colorist ideals on to your child. Stop them mid-sentence in front of your child or loved ones. Correct them and challenge their mind-set and perspective. It may not change how they think, operate, or feel, but it will mean something to whomever you spoke up for.

Another thing we can do to combat this is to hold ourselves accountable to not doing and saying things that reinforce colorism, even in jest. Start being more considerate and cognizant of the fact that what one may perceive as a "joke" in regard to skin tone in our community may actually be hurting someone you know and care for as they silently watch and observe your response or behavior. Be intentional when it comes to your comments and understand you can compliment someone without downing an entire group of individuals who may be aesthetically opposite. Break bad habits and recognize that "light skin, dark skin" jokes, memes, and insults are damaging and triggering for many, and only perpetuate pain and further division among us. Once again, this is why if we want to properly address this thing called colorism, that infects our community, no matter your hue, we must cease playing into light versus dark. Now of course, these things will not magically eradicate colorism, its residual effects, or how institutionalized forms of racism have benefitted using colorist tactics. However, as a community, it is a good start toward healing, understanding, and putting forth the effort to actually break this particular generational curse we call colorism.

REFERENCES

Colorism [Def. 1]. (n.d.). *Merriam-Webster Online*. In Merriam-Webster. Retrieved October 15, 2019, from https://www.merriam-webster.com/dictionary/colorism

Davis, R. (2019, November 6). Lupita Nyong'o talks chatting with Jay Z about her shoutout in Beyonce's 'Brown Skin Girl'. *Essence*. Retrieved from https://www.essence.com/videos/lupita-nyongo-jay-z-beyonce-brown-skin-girl-song/

Grizzle, S. (2018, October 24). Spice made her point—industry insiders weigh in on 'Black Hypocrisy.' *The Star*. Retrieved from http://jamaica-star.com/article/entertainment/2018 1024/spice-made-her-point-industry-insiders-weigh-black-hypocrisy

Johnson, M. (2019, July). Passing, in Moments (the uneasy existence of being black and passing for white). *Topic Magazine*. Retrieved from https://www.topic.com/passing-in-mo ments

Nittle, N. K. (2019, August 15). The roots of colorism, or skin tone discrimination. *ThoughtCo.* Retrieved from https://www.thoughtco.com/what-is-colorism-2834952

Russell, K. Y., Wilson, M., & Hall, R. E. (1992). The color complex: The politics of skin color among African Americans. San Diego, CA, US: Harcourt Brace Jovanovich.

Sanders, S. (2019, June 17). Video director tried to swap out a dark skin model for a light skin model & Tory Lanez wasn't having it. *Hello Beautiful*. Retrieved from https://hellobeauti-ful.com/3028760/tory-lanez-dark-skin-model/

Tharp, L. L. (2016, October 6). The difference between racism and colorism. *Time Magazine*. Retrieved from https://time.com/4512430/colorism-in-america/

Chapter Three

Intersectionality of Attachment Styles and Interpersonal Dynamics

Marcus D. Smith

THE STRUGGLE

It is safe to say there are growing number of millennials frustrated with the state of platonic and intimate relationships. Based on the increase in relationship blogs, websites, and apps, dating and social support appear to have taken a decline in satisfaction for millennials. According to Slater (2013) technology has impacted the new generation's perception on commitment because of the plethora of options accessible by the click of a button on their phones. It is understood if one person doesn't meet an individual's expectations, they can move on to another person without hesitation. However, what is not being highlighted in this perspective according to Slater (2013) is the element of choice in relationships. The ability to choose may be a source of shame given that older generations had limited options regarding friendships and had to choose relationships based on proximity. Another component that should be considered is the impact attachment has on relationships for millennials. This chapter will examine this perspective of dating and relationships and view if the current reflections on relationships are accurate or are they simply products of changes in cultural norms, introduction to intersectionality, manifestations of racism, or introduction to technology and access for millennials. Once these issues are explored, then the chapter can process what resources are available to support individuals navigating these interpersonal relationships.

BABY BOOMERS AND GENERATION X

This chapter considers the context in which previous generations lived and compares that experience to current encounters. Anyone wanting to retreat to a "simpler time" may forget that our elders may not have addressed toxic behaviors in platonic and intimate relationships due to the political and social climate of their time.

According to Hummert, Wiemann, and Nussbaum (1994), difficulties in multigenerational connection may come from the older generation's decline in competence. According to the literature the decline in competence is the result of impairment to sensory processing and memory. As a result, there is difficulty processing complex concepts. This difficulty makes sense as brain functioning appears to be a product of lived experiences. If an individual's lived experience is void of seeing others as manifestations of complex identities understood by intersectionality (McCall, 2005), then it makes sense for an individual to have difficulty to connect to others in the current day. This difference in perspective may resemble seeing others only by their gender, or race, or social class.

Intersectionality in communities of color certainly is a component popular in research that would impact an older generation's ability to connect to others. Intersectionality is understood as the relationship of multiple layers and demographic identities of an individual (McCall, 2005). If before, individuals were viewed solely by their gender, race, or social class, people may be neglected the opportunity to identify any conflicts with other parts of their identity. As a result, individuals are neglected the opportunity to be complex. The absence of intersectionality competence clearly speaks to the reinforcement of discrimination that exists in society today. The interest in providing equity and consideration for marginalized groups could be considered the failure to acknowledge individuals in these groups as complex human beings with complex needs. Instead marginalized groups may be seen as inhuman or vehicles for financial gain (Kendie, 2016). For example, a gay Black man in the United States in the 1970s might struggle to see his life experiences and struggles as a product of gender, social class, race, and sexual orientation. In this example without the language of intersectionality this gay male might only be able to grasp and place energy in the issues related to homophobia from the larger society versus identifying stressors that may be present in gender norms, racial group, and access to resources. Because there is limited language to identify the conflict within these complex identities, a person may be limited to unhealthy mechanisms to cope with societal stressors. Some of these unhealthy mechanisms and manifestations for communities of color tend to be physical illness, alcohol and nicotine consumption, and overeating (Keyes, Barnes, & Bates, 2011). If these physical ailments are occurring for people of color without conscious intent, then it's likely to hypothesize its impact or possibility in tarnishing interpersonal relationships.

Aside from the impact of societal stressors, the absence of intersectionality would certainly contribute to a person's inability to connect with others. For people of color it may be common to view relationships as a transactional exchange—transactional in the sense that new relationships are objectified, serve a purpose, and power imbalances are heightened to secure the transaction. For people of color this may be a reality based on the historical interactions America has had with people of color. For the most part, America's interaction with people of color has primarily been for the financial gain of the country (Kendie, 2016). In the midst of uplift-suasion period, America has grappled how to manage people of color if it appeared they were now becoming equals (Kendie, 2016). Moreover, interpersonal theory states human connection is typically delivered based on a person's pre-existing experience. From that experience a person can act on a desire to receive warmth from others. When that warmth is matched it complements additional interactions (Whittingham, 2017). The use of interpersonal theory brings to light a few questions: Is this ideology likely the experience for people of color in the United States? Have people of color for generations experienced enough warmth as Whittingham states to replicate and maintain healthy relationships? If people of color experience shame and stigma with their identities, are they bound to have difficulty to connect and create healthy attachments with others for generations to come?

According to Smelser et al. (2001) and Kendie (2016), the issues of race and social justice for people of color were most significant and indicative to survival versus placing priority in connecting with another person's complex identities. It is imagined the process in digesting the complexities of a loved one seems impractical in the face of violence that was significant for many people of color during the Civil Rights era. In addition, White Americans consistently used racist rhetoric to describe people of color in order to make profit and control them (Kendie, 2016). If a group of people sees themselves as something less than human, then it is likely for individuals to overlook unhealthy behavior in close relationships.

To expand on the possibilities of human connection for people of color, individuals may become complacent and accept unhealthy behavior as cultural traits and norms for multiple generations. These experiences are commonly seen in generalizations of behavior made by people within marginalized groups. These generalizations can be indicators of internalization. Research understands internalization is characterized by oppression that influences thoughts, attitudes, and feelings marginalized groups hold toward themselves, others within their group, and those who are considered privileged (David, 2014).

Along with this experience of internalized oppression in developing relationships, Baby Boomers and Generation Xers in early development did not get the privilege of infusing internet technology into their daily culture. As a result, older generations may have been limited in their ability to set boundaries and choose connections due to the barriers of access and proximity of diverse relationships. This may have been possible for those with resources to travel and potentially meet others outside their immediate upbringing. However, those who lived in poor neighborhoods might have contradicting experiences or at least fewer opportunities to explore healthy relationships outside of their surroundings. In most cases these communities of low socioeconomic status were synonymous with communities of color (Kendie, 2016). Regardless of socioeconomic status, an individual might have access to radio or television in some capacity. Showing authentic relationships that promoted vulnerability and working through insecurities or conflict were not popular images in culture for earlier generations. The makeup of the majority of relationships and families depicted in media in this time were middle-class, two-parent, heterosexual White couples. If you were an outlier of this family constellation, there were systemic and cultural barriers in support (Kendie, 2016; Boustan, 2016; David, 2014). Limitations in support or guidelines in images from the media, entertainment, art, religion, and academia have clearly made an impact on groups of people in their experience with self-actualization over time. This is evident by multiple movements in assimilation to Western culture for many racial, spiritual, and sexual minorities in the United States. The ideology that everyone had their place and role in society based on one aspect of their identity typically informed youth in generation X and Baby Boomers how their life should be carried out.

MANIFESTATIONS OF RACISM

While this chapter has explored some of the realities for the Generation X and Baby Boomers generations, another component to acknowledge is how relationship development for individuals of color is impacted by racism in the current day. These negative manifestations in relationships can be hard to break until people of color gain their own personal evidence and awareness that it exists and has the potential to be maladaptive. The following lists several factors that should be considered when examining the impact racism has in relationships for people of color.

Competition

Today we continue to see remnants of the great migration from the South that was made by Black individuals in the early part of the century. According to literature, the perception of competition for the Black community increased during the Northern migration as there were limited resources and job opportunities (Boustan, 2016). Also, Black communities are historically primed for specific jobs. Even if they shared similar occupations as Whites, they would have diverging responsibilities (Boustan, 2016). This systemic priming carried on to school systems as well. As a result, today's poor value in education in communities of color can be viewed as a method to ensure the only options for occupation are limited minimum wage positions. If school systems in urban cities continue to have issues with large class sizes voiding students' individualized attention, limited resources, and poor pay for quality teachers and aids, it certainly is likely to foster a generation of youth with limited skillsets and resources to obtain jobs beyond minimum wage (Hauk & Richards, 2019). This spirit of competition prevents a group of people to share vulnerable experiences with one another because of this constant battle of losers and winners (Boustan, 2016). This inability to be vulnerable certainly affects the family dynamic in Black communities, which is essentially where individuals learn to connect with others in their adulthood (Lehman, 2005). This winner-and-loser component for relationships can resemble power struggles that occur, which hinders connections.

Colorism

Communities of color continue to grapple with the ideology of beauty based on early racial hierarchies created in order to create revenue and identify a more inferior group (Kendie, 2016). Skin pigmentation and physical features were and still are associated with dominance and privilege (Kendie, 2016; Carpenter, 2009). Most times the features associated with privilege and dominance were Eurocentric attributes (Kendie, 2016). As a result, people of color continue to struggle with assimilation and becoming worthy in comparison to whiteness (Carpenter, 2009). As a result, people within communities of color even receive privileged or negative treatment based on one's comparison to white features (Carpenter, 2009). According to literature, it helps individuals feel morally good (Carpenter, 2009). Although efforts to reclaim minority beauty are apparent in the increase and visibility of natural hair products for people of color, cosmetic products such as Fenty makeup which celebrates a wider range in skin complexion, and increasing images in the media; it is imperative these moments to celebrate diversity and validate the complexity of communities of color continue and are discussed in early education. Early education along with multiple safe spaces facilitating and celebrating diversity in beauty can be significant in changing the way new generations treat each other in relationships.

Secrets

In connection with the theme of vulnerability mentioned earlier, people of color have struggled viewing themselves as human and seeking support (Kendie, 2016). Since people of color have universally been told that they are not human, have innate capabilities of strength, and have high pain tolerance, new generations of color may have struggled to see themselves as capable of vulnerability or fragility, whereas the White community has been allowed to for centuries. If a person is operating outside of their social norm, it appears obvious in this experience follows shame. As a result, people of color tend to dwell in stigma and self-concealment concerning their emotional health and relating to others (Masuda et al., 2012; Musada & Boone, 2011). Self concealment in research is conceptualized as a method to avoid embarrassment and further stigma from others from their experienced challenges (Musade et al., 2012).

How does one have a healthy relationship with others if they hold narratives of stigma in beauty, have difficulty finding support in others in the community, and struggle to be vulnerable with others? What is left? This baggage communities of color hold is likely some of what makes it difficult to navigate lasting friend, family, and intimate relationships. As a result, it is likely Black Millennials struggle with insecurities and limited trust in building relationships. As mentioned earlier in the chapter, technology may have its benefits in access and choice in regard to relationships, but in some cases technology may magnify these generational challenges passed down from the influences of racism. Instead it's important to support Black millennials to seek technology or media which promotes diversity in Black beauty, encourages strength in vulnerability with loved ones, and celebrates healthy examples of solidarity.

ATTACHMENT STYLE

Understanding one's attachment styles can bring some insight into personal needs in relationships. One's attachment style can also highlight barriers in connecting with others. These times of conflict may be manifestations of low awareness in one's personal needs and another person's inability to meet them. As a result, because of this lack of awareness individuals may run the risk of internalizing failed connections. This internalization may create defense mechanisms in which they project their own insecurities and failed connections on to others thus creating a cycle of failed connections.

On the contrary, as social creatures it is important to have awareness in the following areas: how to receive feedback, preference in affection and fellowship, ability to connect and navigate groups, address conflict, and creating. Konrath, Chopik, Hsing, & Obrien (2014) noted that attachment manifests in the following behaviors such as secure, dismissing, preoccupied, and fear. The study was a meta-analysis which observed college students self-report from 1988 to 2011. According to the results of the study, secure attachments have decreased over the past years. The authors could only speculate social trends impacted the changes in attachment during the life of the study. The study reported that changes in family constellations, increase in divorce rate, and the rise of social media may have played a part in the isolation of human relationships, decrease in empathy, and increase in narcissism (Konrath et al., 2014). It is hoped when readers better understand their pattern in connecting with others, it's likely they can engage in relationships that complement their attachment style versus minimize or create additional conflict.

TOOLS FOR CLINICIANS

In conclusion of this chapter, this chapter highlights three components that can be helpful for clinicians in supporting people of color navigate healthy relationships. These three elements include awareness of maladaptive behaviors, being open to process racial identity and attachment in the therapeutic relationships, and supporting communities of color advocate for healthy examples in the media and community spaces.

The argument that millennials have relationships which lack fulfillment may be a sign of neglected responsibility. This lack of awareness in responsibility is common for anyone, especially when maladaptive behaviors are infused in cultural norms and systemic oppression. As a result, any clinician can choose a number of theories to support clients regain a sense of responsibility in their relationships. Specifically, this chapter highlights Choice Theory, which suggests individuals should reflect and assess whether the methods used to obtain their needs are efficient (Glasser, 1999). This intervention used in therapy emphasizes awareness and individual responsibility. It's possible this responsibility can support clients reorienting perspective, boundaries, and willingness to be vulnerable with others. All these things mentioned are behaviors that start with the individual and not external parties. If a person does not have access and understanding of theory, they can simply use their displeasure in relationships as a vehicle to create change. As a result, this chapter suggests that individuals should delay their reaction to internalize failed connections as a result of their individual character or blame others for being humanly flawed or not meeting their needs.

Along with this need for awareness, readers must acknowledge navigating healthy relationships should not be done in isolation. Learning to experience the full benefits of Choice Theory and maneuver one's personal attachment styles can be a daunting task if done in isolation. Individuals can avoid feeling overwhelmed by being supported with a clinical professional who studies human behavior. These clinical professionals can be a psychologist or licensed professional counselor and licensed social worker. Avoiding help-seeking behaviors might communicate an inability to be vulnerable with others. This lack of vulnerability certainly was one of the manifestations of racism mentioned earlier in the chapter. It assumes the individual should already have the answer to perfect relationships and may risk feelings of inadequacy if they can't figure it out. Based on the historical stigma people of color have toward the medical (Kendie, 2016) and mental health field, it is essential clinical professionals of color immerse themselves in these communities to share their knowledge and personal stories to eliminate experiences of shame and difficulty with vulnerability. Another way clinicians can be supportive in helping clients of color navigate relationships would be exploring their racial identity. Since the majority of this chapter has examined the impact of racism on relationship development, it is imperative clients gain insight where they fall on the spectrum of racial identity (Cross, 1991). Essentially, clinicians can explore with clients in the following order:

Racial Identity

- How has racism impacted their worldview?
- What actions have they taken place to connect with their race and others outside their racial group?

Attachment Styles

- What patterns are present in their ability to connect to others?
- What are their needs in communication, affection, and maintenance?

Direction and Movement with Choice Theory

- What methods have been utilized?
- What possible new solutions could create different outcomes in relationships?

After reading this chapter, it is hoped communities of color choose to engage in alternatives and new behavior to develop meaningful relationships since shaming and retreating to isolation haven't seemed to obtain favorable results.

In addition to awareness and seeking clinical support, clinicians that support people of color in therapy can continue to facilitate safe spaces that uplift healthy and authentic relationships in their community. To add to this idea of exposure and community, demanding images of people of color in

healthy relationship are also imperative to the development of new generations (Jeevanjee, 2008). History has shown how instrumental biased literature, minstrel shows, and depictions of people of color in the media have
normed the way society should treat them and how minorities should see
themselves (Jeevanjee, 2008). As a result, it should be just as impactful to
counteract those negative images with authenticity. Individuals with the resources should place financial support in organizations that value healthy
connections between people of color so that others within the community can
learn and grow from it. According to qualitative research, telling stories and
understanding the lived narratives and experiences of others resonate for
communities of color (Moustakas, 1994). Therefore, communicating a new
narrative of possibilities versus barriers for Black Millennials to learn in safe
spaces, novels and the media can be effective in breaking the perceived
issues millennials experience in relationships.

REFERENCES

Boustan, L. (2016). *Competition in the promised land* (National bureau of economic research
    publications). Princeton University Press.
Cross, W. (1991). *Shades of Black: Diversity in African-American identity.* Philadelphia: Tem-
    ple University Press.
David, E. (2014). *Internalized oppression: The psychology of marginalized groups.* New York:
    Springer Publishing Company.
Gibson, L., & Sodeman, W. (2014). Millennials and technology: Addressing the communica-
    tion gap in education and practice. *Organization Development Journal, 32*(4), 63–75.
Glasser, W. (1999). *Choice theory: A new psychology of personal freedom.* New York, NY,
    US: HarperPerennial.
Harrison, C. (2010). *American culture in the 1990s* (Twentieth-century American culture).
    Edinburgh: Edinburgh University Press.
Hauk, G., & Richards, E. (2019, October 22) *When will the Chicago teacher strikes be over?*
    Retrieved from https://www.usatoday.com/story/news/education/2019/10/22/cps-strike-up
    date-chicago-public-schools-teachers-demands-elizabeth-warren/4064110002/
Hummert, M., Wiemann, J., & Nussbaum, J. (1994). *Interpersonal communication in older
    adulthood: Interdisciplinary theory and research* (Sage focus editions). Thousand Oaks:
    SAGE Publications. (1994).
Internet intimacy: Authenticity and longing in the relationships of millennial young adults.
    (2018). *Sociological Perspectives, 61*(4), 626–641. doi:10.1177/0731121417753381
Jeevanjee, A. (2008). *Diversity in the media: History of the cultural diversity advisory group to
    the media 1992–2007.* Waterside Press.
Kendie, I. X. (2016). *Stamped from the beginning: The definitive history of racist ideas in
    America.* New York: Nation Books.
Keyes, K., Barnes, D., & Bates, L. (2011). Stress, coping, and depression: Testing a new
    hypothesis in a prospectively studied general population sample of U.S.-born whites and
    blacks. *Social Science & Medicine, 72*(5), 650–650. doi:10.1016/j.socscimed.2010.12.005
Konrath, S. H., Chopik, W. J., Hsing, C. K., O'Brien, E. (2014). Changes in adult attachment
    styles in American college students over time: A meta-analysis. *Personality and Social
    Psychology Review*, 18 (4), 326–348.
Lehman, J. (2005). *Understanding marriage, family, and intimate relationships.* Springfield:
    Charles C Thomas Publisher.

McCall, L. (2005). The complexity of intersectionality. *Journal of Women in Culture and Society, 30*(3), 1771–1800.

McGlynn, A. P. (2010, September 6). Millennials—the "always connected" generation. *The Hispanic Outlook in Higher Education, 20,* 14–16. Retrieved from https://tcsedsystem .idm.oclc.org/login?url=https://search-proquest-com.tcsedsystem.idm.oclc.org/docview/751 193424?accountid=34120

Musada, A., Anderson, P., Edmonds, J. (2012). Help-seeking attitudes, mental health stigma, and self-concealment among African American college students. *Journal of Black Studies, 43*(7), 773–786.

Masuda, A., & Boone, M. S. (2011). Mental health stigma, self-concealment, and help-seeking attitudes among Asian American and European American college students with no help-seeking experience. *International Journal for the Advancement of Counseling, 33*(4), 266–279. doi:http://dx.doi.org.tcsedsystem.idm.oclc.org/10.1007/s10447-011-9129-1

Myers, K., & Sadaghiani, K. (2010). Millennials in the workplace: A communication perspective on millennials' organizational relationships and performance. *Journal of Business and Psychology, 25*(2), 225–238.

Smelser, N., Wilson, W., Mitchell, F., National Research Council (U.S.). Commission on Behavioral and Social Sciences and Education, & Research Conference on Racial Trends in the United States (1998: Washington, DC). (2001). *America becoming: Racial trends and their consequences*. Washington, DC: National Academy Press.

Slater, D. (2013). *Love in the time of algorithms: What technology does to meeting and mating*. New York: Current.

Chapter Four

An Examination of the Father-Child Relationship within the African American Household

Natascha C. Dillon

The role of the father is an integral component in the psychological, emotional, and social development of his offspring. To date, few studies have examined the dynamics of the father-child relationship in correlation with healthy development, especially in African Americans. Moreover, the majority of research tends to examine the role of heterosexual fathers; and fails to explore the psychosocial and emotional impact of the father-child relationship within same sex partnerships. Fathers' lack of parental involvement has been linked to emotional, psychological, socioeconomic, and social development deficits in their children. African American youth without actively involved father figures tend to present with greater challenges related to lower socioeconomic status, the significant decline of marriage in the Black community, and the increase of female-headed households. African American children who are raised without paternal involvement encounter higher teen pregnancy rates, poverty, increased incarceration rates, decreased educational attainment, and greater maladaptive behaviors in comparison to their Caucasian and Latino counterparts. This chapter examines the role of African American fathers in the psychosocial development of their children. Moreover, the chapter addresses the quality of the interaction between the father and the child that best promotes healthy development. Furthermore, the chapter will evaluate the functional role of Black fathers in the development of greater prosocial behaviors and outcomes in children. Finally, the chapter proposes interventions and preventive measures that may help to decrease the risk of psychopathology in African American youth.

A number of studies have indicated that the father-child relationship plays an important role in outcomes for children. For example, East, Jackson, and O'Brien (2007) found that lack of paternal involvement was linked to numerous difficulties including health and welfare issues, sexual promiscuity, increased teen pregnancy rates, subpar school performance, and low self-efficacy in the women (East et al., 2007). One major limitation of the study was that the researchers did not identify the race of the women. This information would have been helpful in determining whether racial differences play a role in fathering practices.

A 2009 study of 122 African American teenage girls examined the correlation between the quality of the father-daughter relationship and academic success (Cooper, 2009). Cooper found that conflictive relationships between fathers and their children increase the likelihood of depression, acting out behaviors, and delinquency in school.

Most of studies that pertain to African American father-child relationships have primarily focused on the decline of marriage in the Black community and higher incarceration rates as the catalysts for a father's disengagement and poor paternal involvement (Coley, 2003). A common societal misapprehension is that Black fathers are deadbeat dads. Most studies tend to ignore how low socioeconomic constraints contribute to the marginalization of the male provider, thus resulting in his inability to effectively parent. Thus, this chapter examines the role of African American fathers in the psychosocial development of their children.

EPIDEMIOLOGY

Recent statistics indicate that there is greater need for research on the role of the father, and more specifically the African American father. According to a 2014 U.S. Census Bureau report, 23.6 percent of U.S. children lived apart from their biological fathers (National Fatherhood Initiative, 2010). More specifically, this statistic equates to 1 out of every 3 (33%) children in America. Moreover, nearly 2 in 3 (64%) African American children, 1 in 3 (34%) Hispanic children, and 1 in 4 (25%) Caucasian children live in father-absent homes (National Fatherhood Initiative, 2010). A U.S. Census report published in 1995 found that 54 percent of never married Black fathers and 23 percent of divorced Black fathers are raising their children in single-parent homes.

The presence of African American two-parent homes began to gradually change in the 1960s with the most drastic shift occurring between 1970 and 1980 (U.S. Census, 1993). In 1970, 68 percent of African American households consisted of two-parent homes, and 28 percent were headed by women (U.S. Census, 1993). This is in stark comparison to 56 percent of Black two-parent homes and 40 percent single-mother homes in 1980 (U.S. Census, 1993). The numbers further differ when factoring in geographic location. Southern states, including Arkansas, Louisiana, Mississippi, and Tennessee, hold the highest rates of father-absent African American homes correlated with higher rates of poverty and lower education attainment (Rosiak, 2012). In 2015, there were 9 percent two-parent Black homes and 17.3 percent single-mother homes in Arkansas, 9.3 percent two-parent Black homes and 17 percent female-only headed homes in Louisiana, 10.6 percent two-parent Black homes and 17.7 percent single-mother homes in Mississippi, and 10.6 percent two-parent African American homes and 16.9 percent female-only headed homes in Tennessee (U.S. Census, 2015).

Father absence may also correlate with a father's age and race. Scott, Steward-Streng, Manlove, and Moore (2012) researched characteristics of adolescent fathers to include the father's race, residential status, and their perceptions of fatherhood. The researchers analyzed the data of men who participated in the 1997 National Longitudinal Survey of Youth who conceived their first child during adolescence. The sample group consisted of 490 adolescent male U.S. fathers initially between the ages of 13 and 19 years and concluded the study when the participants were 22 to 24 years of age. The longitudinal study began in 1997 and concluded in 2008. In terms of race, 48 percent of the fathers were White, 29 percent Black, 19 percent Hispanic, 4 percent reported as other. The researchers found that unmarried adolescent parenthood relates to instability in the family dynamic (Scott et al., 2012). Moreover, 49 percent of the fathers conceived more children in their early 20s despite education and economic barriers (Scott et al., 2012). Furthermore, teen fathers who resided with the mother of their first-born child were more likely to remain in the home and actively engage in the parenting experience (Scott et al., 2012). The study provided some information on the perception of adolescent fatherhood; however, the researchers failed to provide specific information on perceptual differences on fathering practices based on race. Furthermore, the researchers did not provide substantial information about how adolescent fathers impact the psychosocial and emotional development of their offspring.

The statistics and the longitudinal study on adolescent fathers may not fully reflect widespread father-absent homes in the African American community. Therefore, it is important to first identify how historical factors have shaped the African American family.

HISTORY OF THE AFRICAN AMERICAN FATHER

In order to understand contemporary African American fatherhood and its challenges, it is important to consider the way this role has changed over generations across history. Historically, African American men have been physically and mentally enslaved, emasculated, economically isolated, and subjected to systemic and institutional racism, impacting their internal and external lives (McAdoo, 1997). However, prior to the institution of slavery, African men were actively involved in the caretaking of their children (Poussaint, 1996). Furthermore, African men attempted to keep their families intact during slavery, and tried to locate and reunite the family after slavery officially ended in the United States (Zinn, 1995).

Black men continued to consistently be providers, protectors, and the head of the Black family until the middle to late 1960s. Prior to the 1960s, most African American homes were comprised of two parents (Wade, 1994). Beginning around 1965, the percentage of intact Black families declined (Feinberg, 1978). Additionally, the percentage of children born to unmarried parents in the Black community rose from 16.8 percent to 23.6 percent; as did the divorce rate, which was 40 percent higher among Blacks than Whites (Patterson, 2015). A number of factors beginning in that decade appeared to play a role in the dissolution of the Black family. These included an increase in the poverty gap between Whites and Blacks, an increase in crime among Black men, and high incarceration rates of Black males (Wade, 1994).

The portrayal of the deadbeat Black father surfaced in 1965 after Daniel Moynihan, Assistant Secretary of the Department of Labor, released *The Negro Family: The Case for National Action* (U.S. Department of Labor, 1965). This report was a successor to his previous report entitled *One-Third Nation*, which documented the percentages of young Black males from single-parent homes who failed psychological assessments for the military draft (Patterson, 2015). With collaboration from the Labor Department, and through researching works by famous Black scholars, Moynihan completed the report in three months (Patterson, 2015). *The Negro Family: The Case for National Action* report claimed that Black father-absent homes were the sole contributor to the dissolution of the Black family, as well as the catalyst for poverty, crime, and the ills of the African American community. Although this report has been contested and severely challenged over the years (Patterson, 2015), the fallout continues to adversely affect the perception of Black fathers and further perpetuates the deadbeat African American father stereotype. Much of the literature pertaining to African American fathers has negatively characterized these men as absentee and financially negligent (Coley, 2001). However, what the literature often fails to incorporate are the historic underlying circumstances that have posed barriers to adequate fathering practices.

Traditionally, the view of American fatherhood is deeply rooted in the Euro-American fathering approach. The traditional Eurocentric model of family consists of a two-parent home in which the father works and the mother is unemployed (McAdoo, 1997). This is not the case in most African

American homes. According a 2015 U.S. Census report, 34 percent of Black children were raised in two-parent households, in comparison to 83 percent Asian, 74 percent White, and 60 percent Hispanic children (Child Trends, 2015). Therefore, the traditional definition of fatherhood may not fully encapsulate the true nature of the Black father's role in the psychosocial and emotional development of his children (Conner & White, 2006). African American fathers differ from White fathers, given that Black fathers tend to have increased rates of unemployment, homelessness, and are often unmarried (Johnson & Staples, 2005). Moreover, in comparison to Caucasian fathers, Black fathers are more likely to reside outside the home. Furthermore, Black fathers may often participate in the fathering experience more often than their white male counterparts, although most Black fathers are not a part of the traditional nuclear family unit (Boyd-Franklin, 1989). Research suggests that more African American fathers are beginning to raise their children on their own, and that noncustodial fathers are just as likely to engage in care-taking tasks, when compared to their white male counterparts (Coles, 2002).

A 2013 study by National Health and Statistics measured father involvement (residential and nonresidential fathers) based on the frequency of the father's participation in child-rearing practices in two groups of children ages 5 years and under, and children ages 5 to 18 years. The purpose of the study was to determine whether father involvement was a predictor of positive outcomes for children.

The men in this study were comprised of 10,403 men between the ages of 15 and 44 years from the United States. In the children-under-5-years group, there were 1,790 residential fathers, and 410 nonresidential fathers. In the children ages 5 and 18 years group, there were 2,091 residential fathers, and 1,075 nonresidential fathers. Data obtained from National Health and Statistics (2013) found that 16.5 percent nonresidential Black fathers of children under the age of five years played more with their children, in comparison to 6.6 percent of White fathers. Moreover, 7.8 percent of nonresidential Black fathers read to the children, in comparison to 3.2 of White fathers (Jones & Mosher, 2013). In keeping with the National Health and Statistics (2013) findings, 17.8 percent of nonresidential Black fathers of children between the ages of 5 and 18 years talked to their children about their day, in comparison to 16.1 percent of White fathers. Furthermore, 9.7 percent of nonresidential African American fathers helped with homework, in comparison to 5.0 percent of Caucasian fathers (Jones & Mosher, 2013).

The major strength of this study was the large national sample size that was representative of both residential and nonresidential fathers. In contrast, the study failed to identify a focal child for each father. Therefore, it is unclear whether the father's involvement differed depending on the child. For instance, a father with a sixteen-year-old adolescent and one-year-old child may be more involved with the caretaking activities of the adolescent as opposed to the child. Thus, the researchers would not have known the level of involvement he had with the one-year-old. Overall, the study found that generally fathers that reside in the home tend to be more engaged in the daily lives of their children more than nonresidential fathers. However, non-residential Black fathers tended to be more engaged in caretaking than their Caucasian counterparts. These finding are important when considering the role that a father plays in the psychological and emotional development of his offspring.

Much of the literature on Black fathers does not fully reflect those that are actively involved in the lives of their children (Bright & Williams, 1996). Although the majority of fatherhood statistics depict a decline in Black father-present homes, Black fathers frequently interact with their children despite not residing in the home (Amato & Rivera, 1999; Gadsden & Smith, 1994). In addition, African American fathers are often excluded from the parenting literature, and the existing literature may fail to address how cultural and socioeconomic factors help to shape the Black father's perception of self, family, and the world (Rane & McBride, 2000).

More recently, researchers are beginning to conceptualize Black fathers through a theoretical approach by incorporating the role of social learning, father-child attachment, and ecological factors that contribute to how a man views his role as father (Amato & Rivera, 1999). The proceeding chapter will review theories and research that help to conceptualize the role of the father in general, and Black fathers specifically.

THEORETICAL PERSPECTIVES ON THE ROLE OF THE FATHER

There are numerous theories and models proposed to conceptualize the role of the father. A number of these theories are relevant to an understanding of the healthy psychological development of African American youth. The five theories that are most important to consider include Identity Theory, Father Child Attachment Theory, Paternal Attachment Deficit Model, the Cultural-Ecological Theory, and the Afrocentric Approach to fathering. There has been increasing literature in recent decades about the role of the father in child development. Current research includes a focus on such contemporary issues as father-child interactions, coparenting interventions, and the impact of father absence (Lamb, 2004). This is much different from early fathering research that viewed fathers solely as breadwinners and disciplinarians (Lamb, 2004). The current literature includes a consensus that positive father-child interactions lead to better psychological outcomes in their offspring (Carlson, 2006).

The paradigm shift in the literature has sparked a push for public aware-ness about the importance of fatherhood, thus resulting in government poli-cies such as President Barack Obama's Fatherhood Initiative Fund (The White House, 2016). In June 2016, President Barack Obama announced a nationwide initiative that would help to raise awareness about the importance of fathers' engagement in the lives of their children (*Washington Post*, 2015). Although admirable, this initiative does not consider the cultural context of fatherhood or the factors that may impede on a father's involvement with his child. Thus, it is important to explore how the role of the father differs across racial and cultural lines.

Identity Theory

Traditionally, the primary role of a father was the disciplinarian and bread-winner (Lamb, 2004). It was assumed that the mother was the nurturer. Research has shown that mothers are more likely to identify parenting as a necessary duty, whereas fathers are more likely to view child rearing as an option (Coles, 2002). The importance that a man places on his role as a father is attributed to how he views himself. Identity theory works to explain this role of self (Coley, 2003).

Identity Theory is a derivative of Psychologist Herbert Meade's concept of Symbolic Interactionism. Symbolic interactionism describes how societal norms shape the way an individual behaves (Stryker & Burke, 2000). Stryker has further expounded on Meade's early work with his concept of Identity Theory. Identity Theory is the principle that societal norms mold how an individual views self, and how their perception of self impacts their behav-ioral functioning (Stryker, 1987). This theory further suggests that identity is formulated through social interactions, and the position that the individual holds during these interactions (Stryker, 1987; Stryker & Serpe, 1994). Thus, each social interaction dictates the person's given identity. For example, an individual may have numerous identities: a spouse, a parent, an employee, and a full-time student. However, if the person identifies most with the student role, they may place school-related tasks at the top of their hierarchy and potentially neglect other identity roles. Stryker (1987) coined the term Identity Salience to describe the hierarchical identity role. In terms of father-hood, Identity Theory works to explain the relationship between a father's identity and his fathering behaviors (Rane & McBride, 2000). Carlson, Edle-son, and Kimball (2014) further explored Identity Theory through their re-search on first-time fathers.

The findings of this study suggest that a father's identity is first developed during an infant's prenatal period. Moreover, Identity Salience was appli-cable when determining where financial stability and caretaking ranked on the father's hierarchy (Carlson et al., 2014). As with most fathering literature,

African American men were underrepresented in the Carlson et al. study. First, Black fathers accounted for only 6 percent of the small sample size of forty-seven men. Second, there was no discussion of culture implications and how these factors may impede effective fathering practices. Finally, the study failed to consider the differences among fathers and how Identity Salience may be different based on internal role expectations.

Identity Theory also suggests that a father's commitment to his child leads to higher Identity Salience (Fox & Bruce, 2001; Stryker & Serpe, 1994). David DeGarmo's research on Identity Theory further explored the correlation between identity and salience as a predictor of long-term fathering involvement. The findings of this study suggest that a father's identity is a better predictor of parenting engagement, and that Identity Salience was an important predictor of the number of father-child interactions (DeGarmo, 2010). Similarly, to the Carlson et al. (2014) study, the number of minority participants was minimal. Moreover, the exact number of African male participants was not indicated in the study. Given that most of the fathering literature is predominantly conducted on Caucasian middle-class fathers, future literature on African American fathers should be viewed through a multicultural perspective.

Father-Child Attachment Theory

Father-Child Attachment Theory is a contemporary version of Bowlby's Attachment theory. Bowlby's research on Attachment theory suggests that a child's mental health is tied to the development of a secure and warm parental attachment during infancy (Bretherton, 1997). According to Bowlby (1979), parents act as bases of security through which a child can examine their external environment. A secure attachment between the father and the child may foster perseverance and self-activation when the child encounters adversity (Kerns, Tomich, & Kim, 2006). Historically, most of the research on attachment focused on the mother-child attachment, but more recently the father-child attachment has been receiving attention. The majority of the research related to father-child attachment is equivocal. Some scholars have found no direct correlation between father-child attachment and a secure attachment (Van Ijzendoorn & DeWoff, 1997). Van Ijzendoorn and DeWoff conducted a meta-analysis of eight studies on the correlation between paternal quality and father-infant attachment in middle-class families. An examination of the studies deduced that father attachment does not shape a child's development to the same extent as mother attachment. Furthermore, a healthy and positive relationship between the father and mother molds a stronger mother-child attachment (Van Ijzendoorn & DeWoff, 1997). Whereas, other research indicates that the quality of the interaction is more important than the amount of time spent with the child (Brown, Mangelsdorf, & Neff, 2012).

Brown, Mangelsdorf, and Neff (2012) found that father-child attachment was higher at age 3 years, and that the quantity and the quality of the paternal interaction increased attachment. Although, the study provided valuable information about father-child attachment, there were significant limitations. Black fathers account for only 9 percent of the sample size. Whereas White fathers made up 80 percent of the total sample size. Moreover, the sample size did not account for lower-income fathers, given that the mean income fell between $61,000 and $70,000 annually. This study reflects the need for additional and more specific studies on the African American father-child attachment. Much of the criticism surrounding Attachment Theory is the focus on the role of the mother as opposed to the father (Pleck, 2007).

Marcus and Betzer (1996) conducted a study that evaluated the link between father attachment in middle-school children (grades 6–8) and antisocial behavior. One major limitation of this study was that the researchers did not fully focus on father-child attachment but also included mother-child attachment, and child-peer attachment. This aligned with criticism on Attachment Theory in that it minimizes the role of fathers. The researchers found a high correlation between decreased paternal involvement and antisocial behaviors to include truancy and assault (Marcus & Betzer, 1996). More specifically, the findings indicated that a negative father-child attachment was highly correlated with antisocial behaviors in both boys and girls. A major limitation of this study was that there was little diversity in the study sample (the participants were 80% Caucasian), and the researchers did not include the percentage of nonwhite participants.

Unfortunately, most of information on attachment is more geared toward the mother-child relationship as opposed to the father-child interaction. Despite the minimal literature, most of the research asserts that children develop very similar attachments to their fathers as they do their mothers (Brown et al., 2007).

PATERNAL ATTACHMENT DEFICIT MODEL

Since the 1960s and beyond, African American fathers have been portrayed as absent, uninvolved, and disengaged (Marsiglio, 2009). Additionally, studies on fathers tend to be based on Eurocentric norms (e.g., married, two-parent household) thus frequently diminishing the role of Black fathers (Coles, 2002; Parke, 2004; Smith Krohn, Chu, & Best, 2005). The harsh reality is that many Black fathers are adversely affected by community violence (Letiecq & Koblinsky, 2004), poverty, unemployment, and low educational attainment (Hernandez & Brandon, 2002). Socioeconomic adjustment is seen as a predictor of paternal involvement in Black fathers. This perspective postulates that Black fathers tend to be less educated and encounter occupational barriers, thus diminishing their ability to effectively parent (Smith, Krohn, Chu, & Best, 2005). Paternal involvement with children tends to be higher if the father holds gainful employment, thus allowing him to provide more financial security (Coley & Chase-Lansdale, 1999; McAdoo, 1997). When considering the deficit model, it is helpful to contemplate the cultural, social, and historical context of the role of the African American father.

Prior the 1980s, the literature on African American fathers was viewed from the lens of the deficit model (Wade, 2004). The premise of the Paternal Attachment Deficit model is that an impoverished father's value and belief systems are significantly different in comparison to mainstream societal norms (U.S. Department of Labor, 1965). This theory tends to generalize and group all Black fathers into one category, thus labeling them as less educated and poor (Smith et al., 2005). Granted, African American men tend to have higher rates of incarceration and lower educational attainment (Kimmel & Messner, 1998); it is important to remember those that do not. Consequently, these inopportune barriers affect father-child interactions (McLoyd, 1990). Often, studies of Black fathers do not include fathers that are more financially equipped to care for their offspring, coparenting factors, and nonresidential fathering practices. A study by Perry, Harmon, and Leeper (2011) found that African American in-resident fathers are more active in the daily care of their children in comparison to Caucasian, Latino American, and Asian American fathers. Comparably, nonresident Black fathers demonstrate the same level of involvement with their offspring as did White and Hispanic fathers (Smith, Krohn, Chu, & Best, 2005).

Perry et al. (2011) conducted research on 617 low-income Black fathers (341 married and 276 unwed cohabitating) to examine whether specific factors of paternal involvement, perceived maternal support, work flexibility, level of religious involvement, father self-assessment, and paternal stress, dictated a father's engagement with his child (Perry et al., 2011). Although this study was solely focused on Black fathers, there were limitations in the research. There was a small effect size in the level of involvement between married and cohabitating African American fathers. Furthermore, the participants resided in urban cities rather than rural communities. Thus, cultural differences between urban and rural fathers could not be determined. Lastly, the study did not account for nonresidential Black fathers.

Paternal Attachment Deficit model does not fully account for the Black fathers who play a major role in the lives of their children (Cochran, 1997). Moreover, this model fails to examine the role of middle–class Black fathers, nonresident Black fathers (Cochran, 1997), and full-time single custodial African American fathers (Coles, 2002). A study by Coates and Phares

(2014) explored the specific factors that are correlated with paternal engagement among nonresidential African American fathers for impoverished communities.

The participants in this study were composed of 110 Black fathers with children ages ten and lower. The researchers found that social support is related to a higher level of parental involvement. Although the study supports findings that nonresidential Black fathers too play role in the psychological development of their offspring, the study was limited to low-income African American fathers.

A study by Coles (2002) attempted to explore key reasons as to why some Black men elect to be single fathers. The study concluded that single custodial fathers' motivation to parent independently was based on parental responsibility, not wanting to further perpetuate the absent-Black-father stereotype, the desire to model positive fathering for their offspring, and the desire to further enhance the father-child bond. Although the research provided another important perspective of African American involvement, the study had limitations. The sample size was too small due to low populations of black men in the United States, and low percentages of single African American custodial fathers.

CULTURAL-ECOLOGICAL THEORY

The dire need for diversity in fathering studies has been widely recognized (Coles, 2002; Cooper, 2009). However, most of the research regarding Black fathers fails to incorporate cultural components (e.g., socioeconomic status, family structure, and cultural contextual factors) that are integral to the role of Black fathers (Cooper, 2009). McAdoo (1993) explained that African American fathers are best conceptualized through the prism of the Cultural-Ecological perspective. Cultural-Ecological perspective is deeply rooted in Bronfenbrenner's Ecological Systems Theory. Ecological Systems theory explores how interactions between a person and numerous social contexts influence social development (Brofenbrenner, 1979). Comparably, Ogbu's Cultural-Ecological model works to explain how environmental factors and cultural beliefs influence human behavior (Stanik, Riina, & McHale, 2013). According to this model, to comprehend the parenting norms of minorities, one must first understand the group's views on success (Ogbu, 1978). Moreover, Ogbu explained that the Cultural Ecological model of parenting is a culturally systematized formulation that is collectively shared throughout the child's daily interactions with parents, family, and individuals within their community (Ogbu, 1978). He further explained that a minority child's idea of success stems from the adults that pass the information down to the child (Ogbu, 1978).

Gordon, Nichter, and Henriksen (2012) applied Ogbu's concept in their study of Black fathers. The researchers studied seven Black fathers' perceptions of fatherhood, and how their concept of fatherhood was influenced by their parents, extended family, and society (Gordon et al., 2012). The study concluded that external influences such as their fathers, extended family and community, the ability to make good choices when faced with adversity, and being exposed to a world outside of the community helped to shape the child's psychological growth and development (Gordon et al., 2012).

There were several limitations to this study. The researchers exclusively collected data from middle-aged fathers, the study did not review the role of nonresidential fathers, the sample size was too small, and the study solely examined the father-son dyad. Despite the study's limitations, the researchers provided an alternative fathering perspective that examined fatherhood based on the black experience. The Afrocentric Approach to fathering is yet another model that explores the role of African American cultural patterns to conceptualize the interworking of Black fathers.

AFROCENTRIC THEORY

Afrocentric Theory helps to explain the complexity of the Black family from a non-Eurocentric perspective. Moreover, Afrocentric Theory promotes self-awareness and not societal views of fatherhood (Taliaferro, 2008). In the Afrocentric approach, fathering is not solely viewed from a father-child dynamic, but from a child-community perspective. This theory examines issues from a collectivistic approach, which includes the father-child, mother-child, and child-community relationships (Taliaferro, 2008). Unlike traditional fathering schools of thought, the father can live apart from the child and still have a viable effect on the rearing of his offspring (Graham & Beller, 2002). Furthermore, this theory is deeply rooted in the concept of "It takes a village to raise a child" meaning that the entire community is also involved in raising children (Cochran, 1997).

Based on the collectivistic approach to this theory, it is important to examine the roles that nonbiological Black fathers and extended family play in the emotional and psychosocial development of Black youth. In the Black community, a father figure often assumes the role of the biological father if a father is absent from his child's life (Black, Dubowitz, & Starr, 1999). Although the concept of the Afrocentric Approach to fathering has been present for some time, there is dearth of research on the theory. A literature review of Afrocentric fathering approaches only rendered articles on Afrocentric life as whole, the need for Afrocentric approaches in social work settings, and a small-scaled literature review on African American fathers in general but not the role of the father (Ahadi, 2015). Thus, more research is needed on the

Afrocentric fathering approach, and the role of the extended family and community (McAdoo, 1993). The Afrocentric Approach is deeply rooted in the idea that extended family members and community social support networks are actively involved in child-rearing responsibilities. The following section further explores the role of extended kinship networks and father figures.

ROLE OF FATHER FIGURES

Extended family, supportive kin networks, and father figures are important to the interworking of the African American family. Father figures are especially important in households headed by single mothers (Jayakody & Kalil, 2002). To date, two studies have examined the role of nonparental father figures in African American children's lives.

Jayakody & Kalil (2002) examined the data of public assistance applicants and recipients to determine if a correlation existed between the presence of a father figure and the cognitive development of children ages 3 to 5 years. Of the 749 participants, 50 percent of the children who had daily encounters with a father figure had increased levels of school readiness (Jayakody & Kalil, 2002). The research also suggested that father figures who assist in caretaking tasks help to reduce the stress of biological mothers (Jayakody & Kalil, 2002).

Although the study demonstrated the importance of social fathers, the study had several drawbacks. The researchers did not provide information on the quality and quantity of the father figure-child interaction. Moreover, the sample consisted solely of residents from a county in Georgia as opposed to a national sample. Lastly, the study emphasized the mother's perspective versus the child's.

Further research on kinship networks also supports the notion that father figures can help to mitigate ill behaviors in Black youth (McCabe, Clark, and Barnett, 1999). The researchers examined the relationship between protective factors (extended family support, father involvement within the nuclear family structure), and the primary caregiver-child dynamic. The results of the study were comparable to Jayakody and Kalil in that kinship social support helped to buffer family stress and acting-out behaviors in youth. Moreover, the researchers found that children who possessed kinship social support networks displayed less shy and anxious behaviors. One major benefit of this study was that numerous people provided insight into the children's behavioral patterns, as opposed to traditional studies that offered the sole perspective of the primary caregiver. Conversely, limitations to the study included the small sample size and the lack of a comparison group.

Taken together, these studies indicate that extended support systems and father figures help to play a major role in the lives of children without actively engaged fathers. However, more research is needed on the role of nonparental father figures in the lives of African American children. Specifically, researchers should work to understand the importance of nonparental father figures and extended kin in moderating maladaptive behavioral patterns in African American youth.

IMPACT OF FATHERS ON CHILD DEVELOPMENT

A growing body of literature indicates that fathers are integral in the physical and emotional development of their children. A review of literature on absent fathers illustrates that children from father-absent environments have lower academic achievement (Gordon, 2016), engage in early sexual activity leading to unplanned pregnancy and adolescent parenthood (Ellis et al., 2003), and may encounter marked deficits in social and emotional development (East, Jackson, & O'Brien, 2007). Qualitative literature also suggests that father disengagement may cause emotional and mood disorders, poor emotional regulation, and maladaptive coping-skill development to include alcohol and substance abuse (Cabrera, Tamis-LeMonda, Bradely, Hofferth, & Lamb, 2002). Further qualitative research indicates that children of absent fathers are more likely to join gangs (Boyd-Franklin, Franklin, & Toussaint, 2001), engage violent behaviors due to a disrupted paternal attachment (Garbarino, 1999), and are more likely to engage in risk-seeking behavioral patterns (Garbarino, 1999). Although research exists about the correlation between father engagement and healthy development, there is limited research about developmental processes of fathering. Moreover, the research on fathers fails to consider the true degree of African American father involvement given that most of these fathers reside outside the home (Coates & Phares, 2014). Given the limitations in the literature, there is a dire need for quantitative studies that are representative of the African American father.

Cognitive and Socioemotional Development

The presence of a father and the quality of the father-child relationship appears to play an important role in a child's development. Studies have negative outcomes in cognitive, social, and emotional development among African American children when fathers are absent.

In terms of cognitive development, Pougnet, Serbin, Stack, and Schwartzman (2011) conducted a study on 138 children and their families to explore the correlation between fathers' presence and cognitive and behavioral outcomes. The researchers found a positive correlation between father-present homes and higher levels of cognitive functioning (Pougnet et al., 2011).

Moreover, the study determined that girls who resided with their fathers tend to have less internalizing behavioral problems (Pougnet et al., 2011). Although the researchers found a positive correlation between fathers' presence and optimal cognitive and behavioral outcomes in their offspring, the study encountered several weaknesses. The sample size was too small, which limited the researcher's ability to explore other variables. These specific variables included the quality versus the quality of the fathering interaction, and whether differences occurred in fathers who were absent from their children's homes and fathers who were completely absent from their children's lives. A study by Flouri (2008) provided an added perspective on the role of residential versus nonresidential paternal involvement.

Flouri (2008) examined the relationship between adolescent psychological adjustment (emotional symptoms, conduct problems, hyperactivity, peer relationships problems, and prosocial behaviors) and resident and nonresident fathers. The researcher found that out of the three father groups (biological residential, biological nonresidential, and residential stepfathers), nonresidential biological fathers had the lowest level of involvement. Furthermore, children who resided with stepfathers reportedly displayed higher levels of externalizing behaviors to include conduct and hyperactivity difficulties. Moreover, nonresidential fathers reported higher levels of parental conflict and psychological distress in comparison to residential fathers and stepfathers.

Several limitations existed in the study. The researcher limited the sample to adolescents, meaning that the findings may not be same for younger children. Additionally, the sample size was heavily concentrated with White males and lacked sufficient diversity. Lastly, the study did not identify specific externalizing behaviors. Carlson (2006) further explored the relationship between father involvement and externalizing and internalizing behaviors.

Carlson (2006) utilized data from the National Longitudinal Survey of Youth 1979 to examine the relationship between paternal involvement and internalizing behaviors (depression and anxiety) and externalizing behaviors (argumentative and difficulty interacting with same-aged peers). The study found that father involvement lessened maladaptive behaviors in adolescents. Furthermore, the study found that the higher-quality paternal engagement increased the adolescent's overall well-being. Lastly, the presence of a father equally decreased internalized and externalized behaviors in boys and girls alike. Like most research, there were limitations to the study. The researcher did not provide an exact racial breakdown of the Latino and African American participants. Furthermore, the study did not have a nonminority comparison group. Similar to Carlson (2006), Harris, Furstenberg, and Marmer (1998) also utilized data from the National Longitudinal Survey of

Youth to explore the correlation between father absence and emotional and behavioral functioning of their youth.

Harris et al. (1998) found that fathers are equally involved with their adolescent offspring as mothers. The researchers also determined that fathers had greater emotional and behavioral involvement with their teenage sons than their daughters. Furthermore, father involvement was a protective factor against low educational attainment, adolescent pregnancy, delinquent behavior, and psychological distress (Harris et al., 1998). There were several limitations in the study, including the heavy concentration of Caucasian children in the sample and the sole focus on children from intact homes. Thus, it is hard to infer the role that culture plays in father engagement. Furthermore, the sample was not representative of current fathers, given that 23.6 percent of U.S. fathers do not reside in the home with their children (National Fatherhood Initiative, 2010).

The available literature on cognitive and socioeconomic functioning suggests that engaged fathers help to mediate externalized and internalized behaviors in their offspring (Flouri, 2008). Moreover, that positive engagement may lead to higher academic achievement (Pougnet et al., 2011). Furthermore, that the quality of the father-child interaction is more important than the quantity of the fathers' interactions (Carlson, 2006).

Academic Functioning

Father absence has been associated with deficits in academic achievement (Domagala-Zzysk, 2006). During the 2011–2012 academic school year, 69 percent of Black students graduated high school, in comparison to 73 percent Hispanic, and 86 percent White students (National Center for Education and Statistics, 2017). Consequently, Black young men are more likely to be incarcerated rather than attend college (Education Equality Project, 2009), and Black girls continue to have the highest U.S. pregnancy rate (National Campaign to Prevent Teen and Unplanned Pregnancy, 2010). As discussed in previous sections of this chapter, father involvement has been found to be positively linked to optimal development outcomes in their children (Pougnet et al., 2011). Moreover, father involvement in a child's educational achievement is positively correlated with the child's academic success (Tan & Goldberg, 2009).

Tan and Goldberg (2009) investigated the differences in parental involvement in school-aged children. The limitations in the study were: (1) the measure of school enjoyment was completed by the parents as opposed to the child; (2) the sample was not representative of the national sample, given that the sample was comprised of middle-class suburban families—thus, the findings may not be applicable to low-income urban or rural families.

Cooper (2009) utilized a sample of 122 Black girls (mean age of 12 years) to examine the correlation between father-daughter relationship quality and academics outcomes. The study found that a positive relationship between a father and his female offspring led to higher academic engagement and greater self-efficacy in African American teenage girls (Cooper, 2009). Furthermore, the study determined that Black girls who perceived their fathers as supportive and communicative reported higher levels of academic engagement (Cooper, 2009). Lastly, African American girls reported that a positive relationship with their fathers increased their level of self-esteem, which also lead to higher engagement in the school setting (Cooper, 2009).

The strength of the study was that the researchers were able to provide more extensive information on the quality of the father-daughter relationship as it related to academic achievement and engagement. However, there were several limitations. First, the participants were not representative of a national sample. Additionally, the researchers did not provide specific demographic information as to whether the single parent home was a single mother or a single father.

A similar study by Gordon (2016) also found a positive link between the role of the father and a child's academic success. The study concluded that father school-related involvement and the quality of the interaction between the father and the adolescent led to greater academic outcomes. Although the findings were encouraging, there were limitations to the study. The self-report measure was solely administered to the adolescent as opposed to the parent and the adolescent. Additionally, the researchers did not identify the nature of the fathering relationship to include whether the men were biological fathers, stepfathers, adopted fathers, or father figures. Moreover, 24 percent of the participants were African American in comparison to 57 percent Caucasian fathers. A higher sampling of Black participants may have further extrapolated racial difference among fathers.

Overall, the literature supports the notion that fathers play an important role in their children's academic achievement. Both the presence of a father and the quality of his involvement appear to be related to school attendance and performance. Moreover, positive paternal engagement helps to promote healthy self-esteem and overall psychological well-being in youth (Cooper, 2009; Pougnet et al., 2011).

Risky Behaviors

Research on African Americans supports the importance of the father's role in adolescent behavioral development. The research indicates that paternal involvement helps to decrease risky behaviors in adolescents. Riina and McHale (2012) assessed data from 134 two-parent African American homes in Atlanta, Georgia, to examine differences between maternal and paternal warmth, and the link between relationship quality and teenage adjustment.

The researchers found that paternal warmth led to decreased risky behavior in adolescent males and females. Additionally, the study found that fathers endorsed higher levels of paternal warmth when the youth entered early adolescence. This finding may suggest that the paternal warmth may fluctuate due to developmental challenges associated with their adolescent offspring. The study had several limitations. Specifically, the self-report measure only had three items. Moreover, the families were for the most part financially stable, which is a rarity in the literature on African American families in general.

A comparable study by LaGuardia, Nelson, and Lertora (2014) examined the relationship between daughters from father-absent homes and the daughter's first sexual encounter. The study found that young women raised in father-absent homes reportedly reached menarche and had sexual intercourse at an earlier age. Moreover, young women from father-absent homes had higher risks of adolescent pregnancy (LaGuardia et al., 2014).

Caution should be utilized when interpreting the results, given that there was no comparison group, and the level of father involvement was not specifically measured. Moreover, the researchers did not provide specific information about the males who resided in the home (e.g., extended family, adopted father, or stepfather), and did not specify the degree of engagement with the male figure. Lastly, the researchers did not provide information regarding race and socioeconomic status. This information would have been useful in the exploration of racial and cultural differences in father-absent homes. Comparably, there appears to be a relationship between disengaged fathers and risky sexual behavioral practices in youth (Ellis et al., 2003).

Ellis et al. (2003) utilized data from two longitudinal studies of 281 middle-class girls from single-mother households (81% White, 75% Black, and 2% identified as other) from the United States and 520 middle-class girls for single-mother households for New Zealand. The study found that early father absence led to higher rates of early sexual intercourse and teen pregnancy. Additionally, teen pregnancy was seven to eight times higher in early-father-absent homes in comparison to later-father-absent households. Moreover, the researchers found that there was stronger evidence on the effects of father absence on sexual promiscuity and teen pregnancy than other mental health issues, including depression and anxiety (Ellis et al., 2003). One limitation in this study was that the questionnaires were solely completed by the mothers and failed to incorporate data from the adolescent girls or their fathers. Secondly, the study did not provide information on the level of involvement with noncustodial fathers. This information would have been helpful to examine the quality versus the quantity of the father interaction.

Furthermore, a study by Bronte-Tinkew, Moor, Capps, and Zaff (2006) also explored the relationship between father involvement and the formation of risky behaviors in their youth. The researchers determined that father involvement was correlated with less risky behaviors (criminal activity and substance use) in comparison to fathers that did not actively engaged with their children. Additionally, father attachment was stronger in male children than female children. Furthermore, activities that cognitively stimulated the child, physical care, warmth, and caregiving tasks were highly associated with optimal cognitive outcomes (Bronte-Tinkew et al., 2006). One limitation of the study was that the researchers did not provided data on the participants' country of origin. This information would have been helpful when comparing cultural differences in parenting practices.

Delinquent behaviors among African American youth are of great importance, given the disparate number of Black youth in the juvenile justice system. Paschall, Ringwalt, and Flewelling (2003) conducted a study on the effects of parenting, father absence, and delinquent peer groups on Black adolescent males. After examining the data, the researchers determined that delinquent behavior was negatively correlated with the mother's parenting or the adolescent peer group. Paschall et al. (2003) found a positive correlation between father's absence and delinquent behavior in their male offspring. Furthermore, the researchers found that Black adolescent males who resided in a two-parent household were less likely to engage in illegal behaviors. Limitations of the study were in the small sample size and the omission of specific measures that extrapolated for parenting practices and styles. Research also suggests that the absence of a father also increases the risk of youth incarceration (Harper & McLanahan, 2004).

The researchers utilized data from the National Longitudinal Survey of Youth to examine the link between father-absent homes and youth incarceration (Harper & McLanahan, 2004). The study found that boys from father-absent homes had higher levels of incarceration. Furthermore, poverty was a predictor of criminal behavior, thus increasing the likelihood of incarceration among the boys. The study had several limitations. The researchers solely focused on nonintact, father-absent, and low-income households and did not account for middle-class nonresidential father homes. Additionally, the longitudinal study failed to capture other extenuating factors (exposure to community violence, lack of employment opportunities, lack of mental health resources, and poor education attainment) that may contribute high incarceration rates.

Taken together, the literature reviewed supports a relationship between the role of the father and the risk of children engaging in risky behavior. Furthermore, the literature illustrates that early father absence potentially leads to early sexual intercourse and adolescent pregnancy (Ellis et al.,

2003). Additionally, high levels of paternal warmth help to mediate risky behavior in both males and female youth alike.

Based on the presented literature, there is evidence to support the importance of fathers in molding their children behaviors. This is extremely important when considering African American families. Yet, there continues to be a need for research specifically focusing on African American fathers due to the cultural differences in parenting practices. Paternal involvement is paramount in the prevention of maladaptive behaviors in African youth (Griffin, Botvin, Scheier, Diaz, & Miller, 2000).

INTERVENTIONS WITH FATHERS

There has been increased attention in the literature regarding the role of fathers, as well as interest in interventions with fathers that may promote psychosocial and emotional development of youth. This chapter will review fatherhood programs that work to improve outcomes in the father-child dyad and the family dynamic.

Coparenting Programs

A nonconflictual relationship among parents helps to foster father engagement (Talbot & McHale, 2004). One of the major goals of co-parenting programs is to strengthen the parenting relationship as a whole. Co-parenting programs may lessen martial conflict and increase relationship quality, thus leading to improved psychosocial and emotional outcomes for the children (Talbot & McHale, 2004).

Talbot and McHale (2004) explored the correlation between marital quality and co-parenting. The study found that martial quality was positively correlated with co-parenting happiness. Furthermore, the researchers found that parental flexibility also helped to promote a harmonious co-parenting (Talbot & McHale, 2004). Lastly, the findings showed that maternal self-control and emotional regulation also helped to foster a harmonious co-parenting experience (Talbot & McHale, 2004). There were several limitations to the study. There was little diversity in the participant pool, given that 95 percent of the married couples were Caucasian. Moreover, the researcher relied solely on self-report measures to determine parental flexibility and control. Overall, the study provided evidence that coparenting can be an optimal experience when both parents are flexible and supportive of each other (Talbot & McHale, 2004). Additionally, positive coparenting may help to foster positive socioemotional adjustment in youth (Talbot & McHale, 2004).

Frank, Keown, and Sanders (2015) examined the outcome of a randomized parenting program that was formulated to increase father involvement and enhance teamwork among the parents. The researchers found that the intervention group reported an improvement in their child's behavior, an increase in parenting practices, and reported less parental conflict than the nonintervention comparison group. One major limitation of the study was that the data was collected based on the parents' self-report. Secondly, the researchers did not provide independent measures that assessed child behavior. Thus, clinical observations may have helped to remedy both limitations.

The literature on coparenting programs shows that these programs may help to enhance paternal involvement (Talbot & McHale, 2004). Additionally, coparenting intervention programs may help to reduce parental conflict (Frank et al., 2015). Furthermore, harmonious coparenting may reduce maladaptive behaviors in youth (Talbot & McHale, 2004).

Parenting Programs for Fathers

Most fatherhood interventions work to improve fathering behavioral practices. For example, Roggman et al. (2004) examined an Early Head Start Program (EHS) that focused on play therapy interventions for fathers. The results of the study found that low-income fathers who engaged in toy play positively influenced development in their offspring (Roggman et al., 2004). Furthermore, the complexity of the play, led to better cognitive, language, and emotional outcomes in the youth (Roggman et al., 2004). Moreover, the researchers determined that the program was moderately successful in enhancing the father's ability to cultivate a quality relationship with his offspring. The authors of the study explained that barriers in the study were caused by two factors: fathers' work schedule conflicts and the father's perception that play activities were best designated for the mothers and children. Limitations to the study included the lack of diversity in the sample and the lack of national sample representation. Additionally, 97 percent of the sample fathers were married. The lack of representation of nonresidential Black fathers in the sample reflects the need for more quantitative research studies specifically for Black fathers.

A study by Howard-Caldwell, Bell, Brooks, Ward, and Jennings (2011) addressed the need for research on nonresidential Black fathers, by examining characteristics of African American nonresident fathers and the relationship between engaging in monitoring and racial socialization with their preadolescent sons. Additionally, the researchers examined the correlation between demographic influences and parenting interventions (Howard-Caldwell et al., 2011). The study found that fathers who were younger, who were better educated, who engaged in race-related socialization, and who exhibited minimal depressive symptoms monitored their sons more (Howard-Caldwell et al., 2011). Furthermore, older fathers increased race-related socialization practices with their sons after completing the parenting skills intervention program. Moreover, fathers in general improved their monitoring ability after completing the parenting skills intervention program. Although the findings illustrate the importance of nonresidential Black father involvement as a protective factor in their children's well-being, the study had limitations. The study was formulated on cross-sectional data; thus, the causality in the relationship among variables was unclear. Moreover, the length of the study was not sufficient enough to determine if the interventions would continue to work as the boys get older.

A similar study by Caldwell et al. (2014) examined whether paternal involvement in the Fathers and Sons Program reduced aggressive behaviors in eight- to twelve-year-old African American boys. The study found that the parenting skill training intervention was efficacious for enhancing fathers' parenting skills. Furthermore, the fathers' satisfaction with the newly acquired parenting skills led to greater paternal engagement with their sons. Moreover, paternal engagement was positively correlated with a decrease in violent intentions in the sons. Additionally, aggressive behavior was lower in the comparison group, and aggressive behaviors decreased among boys in the intervention group. One limitation of the current study was the small sample size. Second, the researchers did not account for maternal influences of the boys' outcomes.

This review of the literature on parenting interventions with father indicates that fathering programs enhance psychological well-being of fathers and their offspring (Howard-Caldwell et al., 2011). Moreover, paternal intervention programs improve the quality of the father-son dynamic (Roggman et al., 2004). Lastly, parenting interventions with fathers help to decrease aggression and violence in youth (Caldwell et al., 2014). Based on the literature on fathering intervention programs, there is still a great deal of work that needs to be done to implement culturally competent fathering intervention programs.

SUMMARY, CONCLUSIONS AND FUTURE DIRECTIONS

Since the mid-1960s there has been growing concern over the role of the African American father and his offspring's psychosocial and emotional well-being. Despite the literature's history of focusing on absent Black fathers, these men are often actively involved in the lives of the children, even when they do not reside in the home (Cabrera et al., 2004). Most of the research on African American fathering tends to be based on traditional Eurocentric standards and depicts Black fathers as uneducated, poor, and disengaged (Roopnarine, 2004). More recently scholars have offered alternatives to traditional theories of fatherhood, by conceptualizing Black fathers from a multicultural perspective (Cabrera & Garci-Coll, 2004). Hence, more research is needed that explores the African American viewpoint of fathering practices, and how the quality of the father-child interaction molds healthy development (Coley & Chase-Lansdale, 2000).

Clinical Implications

The research reviewed and highlighted the history of negative perceptions of Black fathers, gaps in the literature on Black fathers, and the need for a more culturally competent approach when working with African American families. Nevertheless, the literature does support the need to promote and facilitate the engagement of Black fathers in their children's lives. Father disengagement has several implications that affect the psychological well-being of a child, ranging from behavioral difficulties to lower academic achievement (Cooper, 2009).

Ellis et al. (2003) found that children from father-absent homes are more likely to engage in early sexual behaviors and become adolescent parents. Other studies have revealed that children of nonengaged fathers are more likely to engage in maladaptive behaviors such as aggression, violence, and drug and alcohol abuse (Bronte-Tinkew et al., 2006). Moreover, lack of a father may later lead to depression in childhood, adolescence, and adulthood (Harris, Furstenberg, & Marmer, 1998).

There is a vital need for more research on the role of Black fathers that may ultimately assist mental health professionals to conceptualize and for-mulate effective treatment. Thus, future research studies need to focus on the development of early intervention techniques, mentoring programs for chil-dren and adolescents that may work to foster the formation of self-esteem and self-efficacy, coparenting courses that help parents raise self-confident and well-rounded children, and psychoeducation on the formation of mala-daptive behaviors associated with father-absent homes.

Given that African American men are an underserved and oppressed pop-ulation, a fathering intervention program should be tailored to uplift, support, rebuild, and educate Black fathers. After rebuilding the fathers' self-esteem, they can than begin the work to improve and heal the family dynamic (Cald-well et al., 2014). Curriculum for an African American fathering program should provide a wide array of training to include: life skills as a means of decreasing the need to engage in criminal activity due to limited resources, effective communication to help foster a more nurturing relationship between the father and child (Howard-Caldwell et al., 2011), and coparenting groups to create a symbiotic relationship between the parents (Talbot & McHale, 2004); thus allowing the parents to model a healthy relationship for their children.

Mental health clinicians working with African American fathers must be cognizant of the historic and modern impact of racism on Black fathers and how racial oppression impacts the functioning of the African American family as a whole. The research suggests that clinicians should refrain from using nonobjective approaches when conceptualizing Black fathers (McAdoo & McAdoo, 1997). More specifically, mental health clinicians must be mindful of their own biases, and refrain from using stereotypes about African American men and their roles as fathers (McAdoo & McAdoo, 1997). Additionally, clinicians should fully understand how intergenerational fathering practices impact the development of Black fathers (Cooper, 2009). When considering intergenerational fathering practices, mental health clinicians should query Black fathers about their fathers of origin, and their past and present experiences with their fathers (Mirande, 1991). Furthermore, clinicians should understand how socioeconomic factors, culture and race impacts the developmental process of African American fathers and their children (McAddo & McAdoo, 1997). More specifically, if a clinician is of a different race, they should ask the father about his reaction to working with a therapist of a dissimilar race (Connor & White, 2006). Lastly, mental health clinicians should regularly assess the fathers' values related to parenting, family, employment, community, and self (Connor & White, 2006). Gathering this information may help clinicians to better conceptualize fathers, and formulate treatment interventions that are specific to African American fathers.

Limitations of African American Fathering Literature

African Americans have their own unique experiences of family and parenting (Cochran, 1997). Early fathering literature was solely based on Eurocentric norms (McAdoo, 1993), and through the prism of the Invisible Black Father misnomer (Mirande, 1991). Past and present research on fathers fails to incorporate differences among African American fathers (Boyd-Franklin, 1989). Thus, African American fathers who are economically stable, nonresident fathers, and single fathers are minimally represented in Black father literature (Connor & White, 2006). These father groups are imperative given that the majority of Black fathers reside outside of the home (Cochran, 1997).

As previously discussed, there have been few studies that have explored fatherhood through the eyes of the Black father (Coles, 2002), which has caused several limitations when studying Black men and their children. A major limitation in the literature on Black fathers is the lack of research on nonresidential fathers who play an active role in the lives of their children (Amato & Rivera, 1999). Lastly, current fathering literature tends to dismiss the systematic barriers to effective fathering practices in men of color (Gadsden & Smith, 1994).

Future Direction of Fathering Literature

Theorists and researchers have offered differing approaches to understanding the role of the father, and how men in general learn to be fathers. In order to thoroughly understand the challenges and strengths of Black fathers, more research is needed on the cultural and socioeconomic factors (Nelson, 2004). Qualitative research on fathers should reflect the cultural values of the African American family and their community (Cochran, 1997). The Cabrera et al. (2000) essay on fatherhood asserts that fathering literature should incorporate theoretical models that encapsulate diversity factors such as the Cultural Ecological Model and the Afrocentric Approach to fathering. Furthermore, studies of Black fathers should assess variations of paternal involvement to include nonresidential fathers, and how modeled behavior influences fathering practices in the African American community (Masciadrelli, Pleck, & Stueve, 2006).

In terms of qualitative and quantitative studies, there needs to be an increase in the number of Black father participants, as well as an increase in longitudinal studies that examine Black fathering practices over the family life cycle. More importantly, researchers should further explore the Afrocentric Approach and the Cultural-Ecological theory to assess whether the role of extended family and the community helps to decrease maladaptive behaviors in youth raised without a father. Theories on Black fathers should reflect cultural values of Black families and the community; must take into account how political, educational, and socioeconomic factors impact African American fathers; and must account for diversity among African American fathers (Cochran, 1997).

CONCLUSIONS

Though research on African American fathers has historically portrayed them in a negative light as absent and uninvolved in their children's lives, more recent literature is challenging that stereotype and raising new questions about their roles. It is clear that African American fathers are important to their children's healthy psychosocial and behavioral development. Their presence is important, regardless of whether they live in the same home. Beyond mere presence, the quality of their relationship with the children is also important to development. By expanding the perspective on the role of the father, clinicians have an opportunity to promote, support, and facilitate a strong role for African American fathers and positive outcomes for their children.

REFERENCES

Ahadi, H. (2015). Fathering and the Afrikan-centered worldview/paradigm. *Black Scholar, 37,* 2. doi: 1080/00064246.2007.11413390

Amato, P., & Rivera, F. (1999). Paternal involvement and children's behavior problems. *Journal of Marriage and Family, 61,* 2.

Black, M., Dubowitz, H., & Starr, R. (1999). African American fathers in low income, urban families: Development, behavior and home environment of their three-year old children. *Child Development, 70,* 967–978.

Bowlby, J. (1979). *The making and breaking of affectional bonds.* London, England: Tavistock.

Boyd-Franklin, N. (1989). *Black families in therapy.* New York: Guilford Press.

Boyd-Franklin, N., Franklin, A., & Toussaint, P. (2001). *Boys into men: Raising our teenage sons.* New York: Penguin Books.

Bretherton, I. (1985). Theory and assessment. *Monographs of the Society for Research in Child Development, 50,* 39–40.

Bright, J., & Williams, C. (1996). Child rearing and education in urban environments: Black fathers' perspectives. *Urban Education, 31,* 3. doi: 10.1177/0042085996031003002

Bronfenbrenner, U. (1979). *Ecology of human developmental experiments by nature and design.* Cambridge, MA: Harvard University Press.

Bronte-Tinkew, J., Moore, K. A., Capps, R. C., & Zaff, J. (2006). The influence of father involvement on youth risk behaviors among adolescents: A comparison of native-born and immigrant families. *Social Science Research, 35*(1),181–209.

Brown, G., Mangelsdorf, S., Neff, C. (2012). Father involvement, paternal sensitivity, and father-child attachment security in the first 3 years. *Journal of Family Psychology, 26,* 421–430. doi: 10.1037/a002783

Bureau of the Census. (1993). *Black Americans: A profile.* Retrieved July 30, 2017, from https://www.census.gov/prod/1/statbrief/sb93_2.pdf

Cabrera, N., & Garcia-Coll, C. (2004). Latino fathers: Uncharted territory in need of much exploration. In M. E. Lamb (Ed.), *The role of father in child development* (4th ed.) pp. 98–120. New York: Wiley & Sons.

Cabrera, N., Tamis-Lemonda, C., Bradley, R., Hofferth, S., & Lamb, M. (2000). Fatherhood in the twenty-first century. *Child Development, 7*(1), 127–136.

Caldwell, C., Antonakos, C., Assari, S., Kruger, D., Loney, E., & Njai, R. (2014). Pathways to prevention: Improving nonresident African American fathers' parenting skills and behaviors to reduce sons' aggression. *Child Development, 85,*1.

Carlson, J., Edleson, J. L., & Kimball, E. (2014). First-time fathers' experiences of and desires for formal support: A multiple lens perspective. *Fathering, 12,* 3.

Carlson, M. (2006). Family structure, father involvement, and adolescent behavioral outcomes. *Journal of Marriage and Family, 68,* 1. doi: 10.111/j.1741-3737.2006.00239.x

Child Trends. (2015). Retrieved July 17, 2017, from https://www.childtrends.org/indicators/family-structure/

Cochran, D. (1997). African American fathers: A decade review of literature. *Families in Society, 78,* 340–351.

Coates, E., & Phares, V. (2014). Predictors of paternal involvement among nonresidential, black fathers from low-income neighborhoods. *Psychology of Men and Masculinity, 15,* 2. doi: 10.1037/a0032790

Coles, R. (2002). Black single fathers: Choosing to parent full-time. *Journal of Contemporary Ethnography, 31,* 411–439. doi:10.1177/0891241602031004002

Coley, R. (2003). Daughter-father relationships and adolescent psychosocial functioning in low-income African American families. *Journal of Marriage and Family, 65,* 867–875.

Coley, R. (2001). Invisible men: Emerging research on low-income, unmarried and minority fathers. *American Psychologist, 56,* 743–753.

Coley, R., & Chase-Lansdale, P. (1999). Stability and change in paternal involvement among urban African American fathers. *Journal of Family Psychology, 13,* 416–435.

Connor, M. E., & White, J. L. (Eds.). (2006). *Black fathers: An invisible presence in America.* New Jersey: Lawrence Erlbaum Associates.

Cooper, S. (2009). Association between father-daughter relationship quality and the academic engagement of African American adolescent girls: Self-esteem as a mediator, *Journal of Black Psychology 25*, 495–516. doi: 10.1177/0095798409339185

DeGarmo, D. (2010). A time varying evaluation of identity theory and father involvement for full custody, shared custody, and no custody divorced fathers. *Fathering, 8*, 181–202. doi: 10.3149/fth.1802.181

Domagala-Zzysk, E. (2006). The significance of adolescents' relationships with significant others and school failure. *School Psychology International, 27*, 2.

East, L., Jackson, D., & O'Brien, L. (2007). I don't want to hate him forever: Understanding daughter's experience of father absence. *Australian Journal of Advanced Nursing, 24*, 14–18.

Ellis, B., Bates, J., Dodge, K., Fergusson, D., Horwood, J., Pettit, G., & Woodward, L. (2003). Does father absence place daughters at special risk for early sexual activity and teenage pregnancy? *Child Development, 74*, 3. doi: 10.1111/14678624.00569

Flouri, E. (2008). Fathering and adolescent psychological adjustment: The role of fathers' involvement, residence and biology status. *Child: Care, Health and Development, 34*(2).doi: 10.1111/j.1365-2214.2007.00752.x

Fox, G., & Bruce, C. (2001). Conditional fatherhood: Identity theory and parental investment theory as alternative sources of explanation of fathering. *Journal of Marriage and Family, 63*, 394–403.

Frank, T., Keown, L., & Sanders, M. (2015). Enhancing father engagement and interparental team work in an evidence-based parenting intervention: A randomized-controlled trial of outcomes and processes. *Behavior Therapy, 46*.

Gadsden, V. L., & Bowman, P. (1999). African American males and the struggle toward responsible fatherhood. In V. Polite & J. Davis (Eds.), *A continuing challenge in times like these: African American males in schools and society.* New York: Teachers College Press.

Gadsden, V., & Smith, R. (1994). African American males and fatherhood: Issues in research and practice. *Journal of Negro Education, 63*(4), 634–648.

Garbarino, J. (1999). *Lost boys: Why our sons turn violent and how we can save them.* New York: The Free Press.

Gordon, M. (2016). Community disadvantage and adolescents' academic achievement: The mediating role of father influence. *Journal of Child and Family Studies, 25*. doi: 10.1007/s10826-0160380-2

Gordon, R., Nichter, M., & Henriksen, R., Jr. (2012). Raising black males from a black father's perspective: A phenomenological study. *The Family Journal: Counseling and Therapy for Couples and Families, 21*, 154–161. doi: 10.1177/1066480712466541

Graham, J., & Beller, A. (2002). Nonresident fathers and their children: Child support and visitation from an economic perspective. In C. S. Tamis-LeMonda & N. Cabrera (Eds.), *Handbook of father involvement: Multidisciplinary perspectives.* New Jersey: Lawrence Erlbaum Associates.

Griffin, K. W., Botvin, G. L., Scheier, L. M., Diaz, T., & Miller, N. L. (2000). Parenting practices as predictors of substance use, delinquency, and aggression among urban minority youth: Moderating effects of family structure and gender. *Psychology of Addictive Behaviors, 14*, 174–184.

Harper, Cynthia, & McLanahan, Sara. (2004). Father absence and youth incarceration. *Journal of Research on Adolescence, 14*, 369. doi: 10.1111/j.1532-7795.2004.00079.x

Harris, K., Furstenberg, F., & Marmer, J. (1998). Paternal involvement with adolescents in intact families: The influence of fathers over the life course. *Demography, 35*, 2.

Hernandez, D. J., & Brandon, P. D. (2002). *Who are the fathers of today?* In C. S. Tamis-LeMonda & N. Cabrera (Eds.), *Handbook of father involvement: Multidisciplinary perspectives* (pp. 33–62). Mahwah, NJ: Lawrence Erlbaum Associates.

Howard-Caldwell, C., Bell, L., Brooks, C., Ward, J., & Jennings, C. (2011). Engaging nonresident African American fathers in Intervention research: What practitioners should know about parental monitoring in nonresident families. *Research on Social Work Practice, 21*, 3. doi: 10.1177/1049731510382923

Jayakody R., & Kalil, A. (2002). Social fathering in low-income, African American families with preschool children. *Journal of Marriage and Family, 64*, 2. doi: 10.1111/j.1741-3737 .2002.00504.x.

Johnson, E., & Staples, R. (2005). *Black families at the crossroad—Challenges and prospects* (rev.). San Francisco: Jossey-Bass.

Jones, J., & Mosher, W. (2013). Father's involvement with their children: United States, 2006–2010. *National Health Statistics Report, 71.*

Jones, K. (2004). Assessing psychological and academic performance in non-resident father and resident father adolescent boys. *Child and Adolescent Social Work Journal, 21*, 4. doi: 10.1023/B:CASW: 0000035220.56477.19

Kerns, K., Tomich, P., & Kim, P. (2006). Normative trends in children's perceptions of availability and utilization of attachment figures in middle childhood. *Social Development, 15*, 1–22.

Kimmel, M., & Messner, M. (1998). *Introduction in men's lives.* (4th ed.). Boston: Allyn & Bacon.

LaGuardia, A., Nelson, J., & Lertora, I. (2014). The impact of father absence on daughter sexual development and behaviors: Implications for professional counselors. *International Association for Marriage and Family Counselors, 22*, 3.

Lamb, M. (2004). The history of research on father involvement: An overview. *Marriage and Family Review 29*, 23.

Letiecq, B., & Koblinsky, S. (2004). Safe parenting in violent neighborhoods: African American fathers share strategies for keeping children safe. *Journal of Family Issues, 25*, 715. doi: 10.1177/0192513X03259143

Marcus, R., & Betzer, P. (1996). Attachment and antisocial behavior in early adolescence. *Journal of Early Adolescence, 16*, 229–248.

Marsiglio, W. (2009). Men's relations with kids: Exploring and promoting the mosaic of youth work and fathering. *The Annals of the American Academy of Political and Social Science, 624*(118). doi: 10.1177/0002716209334696

Masciadrelli, B., Pleck, J., & Stueve, J. (2006). Fathers' role model perceptions: Themes and linkages with involvement. *Men & Masculinities, 9*(1), 23–34.

McAdoo, J. (1993). The roles of African American fathers: An ecological perspective. *Families in Society, 74*, 28–25.

McAdoo, J. (1997). The roles of African American fathers in the socialization of their children. In H. McAdoo (Ed.), *Black Families* (3rd ed.). Thousand Oaks: Sage Publications.

McAdoo, H., & McAdoo, J. (2002). The dynamics of African American fathers' family roles. In H. McAdoo (Ed.), *Black children* (2nd ed.). Thousand Oaks: Sage Publications.

McCabe, K., Clark, R., & Barnett, D. (1999). Family protective factors among urban African American youth. *Journal of Clinical Child and Adolescent Psychology, 28*, 2.

McLoyd, V. (1990). The impact of economic hardship on black families and children: Psychological distress, parenting and socioemotional development. *Child Development, 61*, 2.

Mirande, A. (1991). Ethnicity and fatherhood. In E. Bozett & S. Hanson (Eds.), References, *Fatherhood and families in cultural context*, 54–82. New York: Springer.

National Campaign to Prevent Teen and Unplanned Pregnancy. (2010). Retrieved July 30, 2017, from https://thenationalcampaign.org/

National Center for Education and Statistics. (2017). Retrieved July 30, 2017, from https://nces.ed.gov/

National Fatherhood Initiative. (2010). Retrieved April 2, 2013, from http://www.fatherhood.org

Nelson, T. (2004). Low-income fathers. *Annual Review of Sociology, 30*, 1.

Obama, B. (2016). *Presidential Proclamation—Father's Day 2016.* Office of the White House. Retrieved July 30, 2017, from https://obamawhitehouse.archives.gov/the-press-office/2016 /06/17/presidential-proclamation-fathers-day-2016

Ogbu J. V. (1978). *Minority education and caste: The American system in cross-cultural perspective.* New York: Academic Press, 1978.

Parke, R. (2004). Fathers, families and the future: A plethora of plausible predictions. *Merrill-Palmer Quarterly, 50*, 456–470.

Paschall, M., Ringwalt, C., & Flewelling, R. (2003). Effect of parenting, father absence, and affiliation with delinquent peers on delinquent behavior among African American male adolescents. *Adolescence, 33,* 149.

Patterson, J. (2015). The Moynihan report. *Wiley Blackwell Encyclopedia of Race, Ethnicity, and Nationalism.* doi: 10.1002/9781118663202.wberen019

Perry, A., Harmon, D., & Leeper, J. (2011). Resident black father involvement: A comparative analysis of married, unwed, cohabitating fathers. *Journal of Family Issues, 33,* 6.

Pougnet, E., Serbin, L., Stack, D., & Schwartzman, A. (2011). Fathers' influence on children's cognitive and behavioural functioning: A longitudinal study of Canadian families. *Canadian Journal of Behavioural Science, 43,* 3. doi: 0008-400X/11/$12.00

Poussaint, A. (1996). Foreword. In A. Willis (Ed.), *Faith of our fathers* (pp. xiii–xx). New York: Dutton.

Rane, T., & McBride, B. (2000). Identity theory as a guide to understanding fathers' involvement with their children. *Journal of Family Issues, 23,* 347–366.

Riina, E., & McHale, S. (2012). The trajectory of coparenting satisfaction in African American families: The impact of sociocultural stressors and supports. *Journal of Family Psychology, 26*(6), 896–905. doi:10.1037/a0030055

Roggman, L., Boyce, L., Cook, G., Christiansen, K., & Jones, D. (2014). Playing with daddy: Social toy play, early head start, and developmental outcomes. *Fathering, 2,* 83.

Roopnarine, J. L. (2004). African American and African Caribbean fathers: Level, quality, and meaning of involvement. In M. Lamb (Ed.), *The role of the father in child development* (4th ed., pp. 58–97). New Jersey: John Wiley & Sons, Inc.

Rosiak, L. (2012). Fathers disappear from households across America: Big increase in single mothers. *Washington Post.* Retrieved on July 30, 2017, from http://www.washington times.com/news/2012/dec/25/fathers-disappear-from-households-across-america/

Scott, M. E., Steward-Streng, N. R., Manlove, J., & Moore, K. A. (2012). The characteristics and circumstances of teen fathers: At the birth of their first child and beyond. Child Trends Research Brief, No. 2012-19. Child Trends: Washington, DC. Retrieved from http://www.childtrends.org/wp-content/uploads/2013/03/Child_Trends-2012_06_01_RB_TeenFathers.pdf

Smith, C., Krohn, M., Chu, R., & Best, O. (2005). African American fathers: Myths and realities about their involvement with their firstborn children. *Journal of Family Issues, 26,* 975. doi: 10.1177/0192513X05275421

Stanik C., Riina E., & McHale S. (2013). Parent-adolescent relationship qualities and adolescent adjustment in two-parent African American families. *Family Relations: An Interdisciplinary Journal of Applied Family Studies, 62,* 4.

Stryker, S. (1987). *Self and identity: Psychosocial perspectives.* John Wiley & Sons Ltd; 89–103.

Stryker, S., & Burke, P. (2000). The past, present, and future of an identity theory. *Social Psychology Quarterly, 63,* 254–297.

Stryker, S., & Serpe, R. (1994). Identity salience and psychological centrality: Equivalent, overlapping, or complementary concepts? *Social Psychology Quarterly, 57,* 16–35.

Talbot, J., & McHale, J. (2004). Individual parental adjustment moderates the relationship between marital and coparenting quality. *Journal of Adult Development, 11,* 3.

Taliaferro, J. 2008. *Intergenerational community organizing. Social work practice with African-American families—An intergenerational perspective,* pp. 169–193. New York: Routledge.

Tan, E., & Goldberg, W. (2009). Parental school involvement in relation to children's grades and adaptation to school. *Journal of Applied Developmental Psychology, 30,* 4.

U.S. Census Bureau. (1993). Retrieved on July 20, 2017, from https://www.census.gov/prod/1/statbrief/sb93_2.pdf

U.S. Census Bureau. (2015). Retrieved on July 20, 2017, from https://factfinder.census.gov/faces/tableservices/jsf/pages/productview.xhtml?src=bkmk

U.S. Department of Labor. (1965). Retrieved on July 20, 2017, from https://www.dol.gov/oasam/programs/history/webid-meynihan.htm

Van Izendoorn, M. H., & De Wolff, M. S. (1997). In search of the absent father—meta-analyses of infant-father attachment: A rejoinder to our discussants. *Child Development, 68,* 604–609. doi:10.2307/1132112

Wade, J. (1994). African American fathers and sons: Social, historical, and psychological considerations. *The Journal of Contemporary Human Services, 75*(9), 561–570.

Wilson, K., & Prior, M. (2011). Father involvement and child well being. *Journal of Pediatric Child Health, 4,* 7. doi: 10.1111/j.1440-1754.2010.01770

Zinn, H. (1995). *A people's history of the United States 1492–Present.* New York: Harper's.

Chapter Five

Slicker Than Your Average

Understanding the Young Black Professional

Vannesia Darby

All generations are not created equal, and neither are the racial subsets within each peer group. Yet, many organizations continue to use traditional management practices in a blanketed approach to yield peak performance from their employees, neglecting historical cultural, racial, and demographic differences. With five generations currently coexisting in the workplace, traditional operating procedures are symbolically busting at the seams following a perceived disturbance from one particular group: Generation Y (Millennials). Representative of those persons born between 1985 and 1999, Millennials bring a distinct contrast of employee satisfaction from those within their previous and subsequent cohorts (Alsop, 2008). These altered ideals, coupled with current access to formerly privileged educational and monetary opportunities, have allowed Millennials at large to be perceived as entitled, disloyal, and selfish by their predecessors. The lack of cultural competences also gives way for employers to assume that their superiors, peers, and subordinates of African descent are enraged, one-sided, and unwilling to compromise.

From technology to terrorist attacks, there have been a plethora of events to impact the world on a global scale. Although society within each generation experienced its share of both advancements and issues, the impact of each subsequently caused extremely different worldviews, particularly for the Black Millennials in today's workplace.

Unlike their successors Generation Z, who never experienced life without the internet, Millennials are the generation who grew up with and into the technology boom (Turner, 2015). Additionally, major culture shifts impacting the economy (2008 recession, rising college tuition costs, etc.), the use of technology (the internet, social cell phones, social networking, etc.), and issues surrounding safety and security (school shootings, terrorist attacks, etc.) within the past three decades are integral pieces of their human experience. The use of social media in particular allows for the amplification of the disparity and inequity among cultures, primarily those of African descent.

With regard to Black Millennials within the United States and of African descent, there is also a constant underbelly of racism due to the impact of the eras of disenfranchisement and slavery. While conducting twenty-three interviews with Black professionals, Associate Professor Adia Harvey Wingfield noted that countless studies indicate racism continues to shape many and/or most components of life for Black Americans (Wingfield, 2007).

This disparity is also seen within the field of education. Highlighting the sentiments of Black Millennials in the workforce, Princeton Theological Seminary presented its findings from their Slavery Audit in 2018. The result proved that Princeton's forefathers overwhelmingly contributed to donations to the school, funds for the development of the university, and the economy with dollars garnered off the literal backs of African slaves (Barnes et al., 2018). With this certainty, the Seminary agreed upon an immediate implementation of scholarships to the decedents of slaves, a $27 million-dollar endowment, and over twenty additional forms of reparations (Pride, 2019).

For the Black Millennial professional, events like these must not be ignored as they are critical to how individuals show up in the workplace and world. Additionally, employers should not assume the negative narratives applied to Millennials and/or Black Millennials without seeking to understand the empirical data debunking those assumptions, the culture of the individual, and the events impacting their identity in the workplace. This chapter seeks to refute and add context to those conversations, highlight shared tendencies and habits, and examine the worldviews currently shaping the young, Black professional in a conscious society.

THE GENERATIONS DEFINED

To fully understand both the differences and similarities Black Millennials have compared to their non-Black counterparts, it is imperative for the author to first define the parameters of each generation. For the construct of this article, we will use the following framework: Generation Z (born mid-1990s to early 2000s), Generation Y (born mid-1980 to 2000), Generation X (born 1965–1979), Baby Boomers (born 1946–1964), and Traditionalists (born 1925–1945).

Generation Z: The Post-Millennial Generation

As mentioned in previous works by the author, Generation Z is the generation following the Millennials and can also be referred to as the "iGeneration" or "Post-Millennials." Although commonly and mistakenly joined together with their Millennial precursors, this group has experienced its own share of cultural differences shaping their worlds. The oldest members of this generation currently are tapping out of their teenage years; many beginning the employment search or post-college activities. As noted in previous research conducted by the author, this generation outnumbered both Millennials and Baby Boomers and accounted for 25 percent of the entire U.S. population as of 2015 (Darby and Morell, 2019).

Having never experienced life without the internet, the author's research concludes that this generation longs for human connection and diversity within their group. Additionally, they have been on the receiving end of macro issues such as the September 11 attacks against the United States, the 2016 presidential election, inflation within tuition costs and costs of living, the increase of college debt, and the economic recovery following the 2008 recession (Darby and Morrell, 2019). Thus, their ideals within the workplace are much riskier than those of their counterparts, selecting workplaces that are in alignment with their values and not their salary.

Additionally, Generation Z prefers to be entrepreneurs rather than to maintain loyalty to their employer or to build a legacy with someone else's company. The author proposes that the link between the desire of members of Generation Z to build their own companies is due in part to the technological advances that have been around since their birth. The internet, smart phones, and social media have allowed access to traditionally closed channels of education, equipment, human connections, and advertisement that were once exclusive for companies with large capital. With this now low (nearly nonexistent) barriers to entry, it is fair to see why this generation prefers their passion to guide their professional decisions rather than their paycheck.

Generation Y: The Millennial Generation

Represented by eighty million people, one of the most controversial cohorts are the Millennials. With common nicknames such as the "Trophy Kids" and "Generation Me," this group was already typecasted by the forerunners of their time. Previous research conducted by the author concluded that contrary to the perceptions placed on Millennials, the group is extremely talented, optimistic, and well educated (Darby and Morrell, 2019).

Much like Generation Z, technology also plays a pivotal role in the lives of Millennials and their definition of connectivity. Although this generation can also remember life in the pre-existing digital era, they have also grown into the use of technology and incorporate it into their everyday lives. Researchers Gibson and Sodeman also add that "Millennials expect technology to play a large role in the learning process by allowing access to vast areas of informational sources to be incorporated into the actual delivery of knowl-edge through multimedia modes with an emphasis on entertainment during the learning process" (Gibson & Sodeman, 2014).

In addition to the vast technological advances within this generation, major events impacting Millennials run the gamut. Previous research from the author notes that those events include but are not limited to school shoot-ings such as the 1999 Columbine High School Massacre and the 2008 Vir-ginia Polytechnic Institute and State University Massacre, the 2001 Enron scandal, the 2011 Terrorist Attacks and War on Terrorism, and the 2008 economic recession (Darby & Morrell, 2019).

With this generation growing up with these major events, advancements in technology and heavy uses of standardized tests at an early age, it is logical to see why they consider their careers to be more self-directed. Re-search also concluded that early experiences of multitasking and extracurric-ular activities for this group rewarded effort and participation, rather than merit alone. Thus, when in the workplace, Millennials look for constant feedback from their superiors and strive for work-life balance with any em-ployer. Rather than seeking to be purely entrepreneurial like their successors in Generation Z, Millennials desire to "have their cake and eat it too" when it comes to their professional endeavors. This generation seeks to build parallel careers, keeping their full-time job while also building their own business or brand alongside their traditional tenure. This self-confidence to build their own business can often be misinterpreted as arrogance or entitlement. It would benefit employers to distinguish between the two, as many millennials are high performers in the workplace (Darby & Morrell, 2019).

Generation X: The Latchkey Generation

Generation X is another generation that is often miscategorized. The smallest group within the five sects, this group is extremely self-sufficient. Research shows that this generation experienced an interruption of the traditional fami-ly structure, with many children experiencing the divorce of their parents, being home by themselves, and/or being enrolled in daycare (Clark, 2017). Due to this independent and sometimes distant persona, Generation X, simi-lar to Millennials, are known to challenge authority. In the workplace, they learned to adapt to technology in an effort to not be replaced. With major events such as the Oklahoma City Bombing and the AIDS epidemic occur-ring during their generation, this group values the ability to build a career over time in various places with different employers (DeBard, 2014).

Baby Boomers: The Boomer Generation

The most overwhelming similarities between generations occur between the Baby Boomers and the Millennials. Similar to Millennials growing up in the War on Terrorism, Boomers grew up in the era of Vietnam and the hippie movement (Darby & Morrell, 2019). Additionally, the same connectivity that social media and technology brought to the Millennials were also experienced by this generation with the creation of the television. Major events such as Neil Armstrong's first steps on the moon were seen by an estimated 600 million people, according to a CNN study (CNN, 2019).

Additionally, they are known for having confidence within themselves in the workplace, taking charge, and even challenging authority because of their competitive nature (Debard, 2014). With regard to work and home life, traditional gender roles became a little fluid in this era as both men and women started to go to work. Unlike their Millennial coworkers, however, Boomers place high value in job titles, corner offices, and intertwine their personal identity with their job (Alsop, 2008).

The author concludes that some of the issues occurring in today's workplace between the Boomers and the Millennials are due to the fact that there are many similarities between the two generations, including their ability to be strong-willed.

Traditionalists: The Silent Generation

Just as the name suggestions, the Traditionalists represent many status quo and outdated opinions on political, sexist, and racial matters. Much literary support depicts this generation as loyal and dependable to their employer. They seek to build a legacy and are highly respectable of authority. Events such as The Cold War, The Great Depression, World War II, and the beginning of the Civil Rights Movement divided this generation, one that is very comfortable discussing their political views in public (Darby & Morrell, 2019). In comparison to the Millennial generation, the polarity of the two groups can be seen as extreme. Many members of this cohort are currently retiring.

THE IMPACT OF THE DISENFRANCHISEMENT OF BLACK PROFESSIONALS

With the explanation of each generation now defined, it is imperative that employers understand the underlying currents at play apart from and inclusive of race. In particular to Black professionals, the systematic disenfranchisement woven within the generational subsects cannot be overlooked.

Black Millennial professionals are now working to close the gaps of inequity and inequality that were opened in previous generations. The historical denial and segregation of Blacks in the areas of education, real estate, mental health, public policy, and employment in particular set the breeding ground for generations of Black professionals to continually be marginalized. Employers must recognize that the tools for success for the high performing, young, Black professionals *are different* and value the intersectionality of their education, experience, and race within their professionalism. The author suggests that education, experience, and race exponentially impacts their work ethic, attentiveness, motivation, and output—particularly in workplace environments where racism is not called out or stopped.

According to a study published in *The Journal of Negro Education*, "African American adolescents respond to racial discrimination, particularly educational and occupational discrimination, indifferent ways. Whereas one response may be mental withdrawal and lack of achievement effort (Ogbu, 1978; 1988), another response, rarely addressed in the literature on Black student achievement, may be a strong racial identity and a commitment to academic and professional success" (Sanders, 1997).

In many areas, the "isms" within the Black Millennial culture have been amplified due to the climate of police brutality, social and racial injustice, voter oppression for youth and minorities, and the rise of social and political movements such as #BlackLivesMatter. Coupling these highly sensitive issues with the previous nature of each generation and access to information and resources, Black Millennial professionals have become the forerunners of many grassroots social movements impacting policy change and work culture.

CONCLUSION

The young Black professional is a very multifaceted individual, but not entirely due to desire alone. World events and previously placed infrastructures of exclusion set forth by their non-Black forerunners have subsequently shaped their worldview. Despite the challenges, Black Millennials have risen and will continue to create opportunities for equity and innovation that previous members within their cultural lineage were not allowed to.

The author concludes that in order for employers to yield the optimal level of performance from young Black professionals, they should seek to acknowledge and understand the identity of the Black Millennial and strive to create a safe culture of acceptance. Additionally, employers should seek to understand and motivate these individuals based upon their corporate values, rather than an outdated employee reward system.

REFERENCES

Alsop, R. (2008). *The trophy kids grow up: How the millennial generation is shaking up the workplace*. San Francisco: Wiley.

Barnes, C., Day, K., Henke, K., Kay, J., Mikoski, G., Moorhead, J., Moss, K. Pierce, Y., & Stewart, A. (2018, September 27). Princeton Seminary and slavery. Retrieved December 6, 2019, from https://slavery.ptsem.edu/

Clark, K. R. (2017). Managing multiple generations in the workplace. *Radiologic Technology, 88*(4), 379–396.

CNN, First moon landing fast facts. (2019, August 8). Retrieved December 6, 2019, from https://www.cnn.com/2013/09/15/us/moon-landing-fast-facts/index.html

Darby, V., & Morrell, D. (2019). Generations at work: A review of generational traits and motivational practices impacting Millennial employees. *Drake Management Review, 8*(1/2). Retrieved from http://faculty.cbpa.drake.edu/dmr/0812/DMR081201R.pdf

Debard, R. (2004). Millennials coming to college. *New Directions for Student Services, 2004*(106), 33–45. doi: 10.1002/ss.123

Gibson, L., & Sodeman, W. (2014). Millennials and technology: Addressing the communication gap in education and practice. *Organization Development Journal, 32*, 63.

Pride, N. (2019, October 21). Princeton Theological Seminary announces plan to repent for ties to slavery. Retrieved December 6, 2019, from http://gather-story.ptsem.edu/princeton-theological-seminary-announces-plan-to-repent-for-ties-to-slavery

Sanders, M. (1997). Overcoming obstacles: Academic achievement as a response to racism and discrimination. *Journal of Negro Education, 66*, 83. doi: 10.2307/2967253

Turner, A. (2015). Generation Z: Technology and social interest. *The Journal of Individual Psychology, 71*(2), 103–113.

Wingfield, A. (2007). The modern mammy and the angry Black man: African American professionals' experiences with gendered racism in the workplace. *Race, Gender & Class, 14*(1/2), 196–212. Retrieved from www.jstor.org/stable/41675204

Chapter Six

Branding

Do You?

Lelia E. Ellis-Nelson

Discussing the intricacies of what it takes to build a professional identity, develop a brand, and focus directly on the business aspect of therapy is fairly new within the field of mental health. Some programs have begun to develop ways to incorporate professionalism and business development into their non-I|O and Business psych programs, though they are not fully actualized. As more clinicians begin to see themselves as a business, the push toward autonomy should be met with opportunities for education and support.

Often mental health professionals find themselves on the other end of discussions about low wages, burnout, a lack of resources for themselves and clients, the enduring legacy of how to logistically support themselves under the weight of their own empathy, and the realities of how the field is seen in society. A more direct look into the basic needs associated with the work of master's and doctoral level clinical mental health professionals is a must. Tangible resources and opportunities for our professional development should come in the form of Continuing Education Units (CEUs), required coursework during graduate studies programs, advanced elective courses for those that choose to go further, and regular structured and unstructured group events that provide a space for individuals to discuss their branding needs.

Students should complete their graduate degrees with an understanding of what's necessary to succeed as a businessperson. There should be direct overviews on how to properly set up one's own private practice—a discussion which should include, but should not be limited to, filing taxes, incorporating the name of their business, best practice and creative means of marketing, and the influence of working relationships with other professionals as a means of building a referral base. There should also be a centered focus on how to best represent yourself in your work, so far as it also stands as a true answer to the question, "What will working with you accomplish?" Yali Saar, CEO of Tailor Brands, told Forbes, "Your vision was created to solve a problem or answer a need, so instead of asking whether or not your brand represents you first, ask yourself whether or not it represents your clients and the reason they need your service" (DeVries, 2018). The balance between the *self* and the *practice* is essential due to the nature of fit when taking on new clients for therapeutic, consultation, assessment, and other service opportunities.

For example, the desire to create an open cultural counterspace for Black and Brown mental health and helping professionals in order to directly work on their own personal and professional development is a result of thirty-two years of lived experience as a Black woman. That experience made it imperative to carve out any opportunity to directly take care of the social-political-emotional needs that come with the intersection of the author's identities in a field that is predominantly White. The problem, as Saar posited, is that even within the field of psychology, privilege has a seat at the head of the proverbial table. In order to combat that privilege and work toward a place of peace for helping professionals—like this author and others—there has to be a space available to address the unique concerns related to the richness of their melanin and push toward self-actualization. The balance of the self-existence within those identities—and the practice—how those identities impact one's ability to connect to the work and others on a holistic level—correlates directly to the solution of the problem—Coffee Hour Chicago; unapologetically taking up space as Black and Brown persons to fellowship and increase the necessary competencies to be better professionals and individuals in an otherwise homogenously White field.

The focus of the Coffee Hour Chicago brand is the intersection of racial and ethnic identity with social work, psychology, clinical nursing, and clinical medical practice. The colloquialism, "Coffee Hour," was taken from this author's membership within the Black Baptist church, where Coffee Hour serves as the time between morning and afternoon worship services. During that time, parishioners have the opportunity to fellowship with their peers to talk about their personal concerns and issues impacting them as church members. Fostering that spirit of openness and peace brought on by cultural familiarity led to the term's usage as the title of the organization. The initial thought when conceptualizing the brand development for the organization was to continually ingrain the ideals of community building, shared space, and a common core understanding of the central nuances impacting a subset of the mental health field.

Everything from the marketing materials to the topics and hosts presented reflects that push toward personal and professional fellowship. Using the color brown is not only a nod to coffee itself, but to the variance in skin tone of the members. Showing the faces of those involved makes it personal, individuals can see themselves in the welcoming faces of the promotional materials, and it garners a sense of comfort in the viewer knowing that this will be a space one can call their own. In this opportunity to fellowship, members have a real opportunity to grow interpersonally and professionally. Coffee Hour Chicago meets monthly to address topics ranging from sitting with the discomfort of feeling othered among their peers, paneling with insurance agencies, and the intricacies of using modern therapeutic methods in treatment with clients who belong to multiple marginalized communities. Members have the ability to lead topics of interest, suggest meeting locations, and collaborate with the Coffee Hour founder to find authentic ways to network. Member-led opportunities is further proof of a desire toward giving these individuals a space that's their own, controlled by them, and tailored toward their specific needs.

For now, Coffee Hour Chicago membership is free, but due to the service it provides to the community, it often leads to opportunities that have both financial and professional gains. Its brand recognition for people of color in name alone is enticing enough to have potential members research its purpose further. The look and feel of its social media pages and website make its purpose clear. The hosts' push for opportunities to explore eateries around the city also make it accessible to a diverse grouping of participants. The group in its entirety follows the outlined principles discussed in this chapter: personal growth, professional development, self-care as a means of preventing burnout, and providing opportunities to help others achieve their goals of developing their own spaces.

The hosts of Coffee Hour Chicago actively work toward bettering the brand on a regular basis as they learn more about what's important to their members, potential members, and the fields they serve. Growing in their competency is a must, and necessary for brand survival. Finding ways to continually educate themselves about the best ways to support the organization as a whole directly impacts members' abilities to connect to their own individual work. In a sense, recognizing that having everything figured out in the beginning isn't a requirement for branding and professional development. It is imperative that early career mental health workers come from a place of recognizing their own growth edges as a person and as a business so that they can continue to push themselves toward being a better version of themselves than they were the day before. As early mental health workers pursue their own opportunities for growth in branding, it is important that they give themselves permission to not only fail, but to celebrate their success along the way, and open themselves up to opportunities to share their journey with others. This need of community building will not only help them pursue their goals, but it may also bolster creativity, drive, and business acumen within the field.

DEEP DIVE: COFFEE HOUR

The process of developing Coffee Hour into a comprehensive brand was challenging. The basis of the idea was fruitful, but logistically, work had to be done in order to ensure its vitality. When considering the ways in which it would be most advantageous to begin the process of brand development for Coffee Hour, the author took several things into consideration:

- The author's personal values related to the endeavor and the inherent value the organization would bring to the field.
- How to properly market the endeavor; leveraging social media, the author's networking ability, and how the author functions as an ambassador for the brand.
- Utilizing past and present relationships to inform any growth edges to developing the business necessary by connecting with mentors, past supervisors, and consulting with peers.
- Understanding the author's sense of self, and the impact that has on the entire endeavor.

Considerations for these areas will be addressed in the following. The reader then has the ability to see its applicability to current or future endeavors, with ideas on how to utilize one's resources in order to build a successful brand.

Values

Given that the social-political climate is constantly changing, it is necessary that each individual take the responsibility to take inventory of what's important to them—especially within the realm of professional development. There is a direct link between what a person values, how they see themselves, and the type of work they are willing to put into their own growth. For instance, a clinician who values healthy interpersonal relationships would make it a priority to send "thank you" letters to those they've interviewed with and/or met with for consultation purposes. However, because of the change in society the resources to uphold that value varies. There is an option for there to be a formal thank you note in the form of a card with a handwritten message mailed to the individuals preferred address, an email sent to their professional email (if available), or a text message depending on level of familiarity. In each instance, the clinician is showing their appreciation for another professional's willingness to take time out of their schedule to assist them with the acquisition of new employment, improving their services through consultation, providing them with information that would assist them along the pursuit of connecting more intimately with their sense of self, and so forth.

Martin Fishbein (1970) posited that "a person's behavior is determined by how highly a goal is valued, and by the degree to which the person expects to succeed."

MOTIVATION = EXPECTANCY X VALUE

Considering Fishbein, helping professionals have the responsibility to consider their short- and long-term goals as they relate to their personal and professional lives. It allows them an opportunity to take in the tangible results of their dedication and labor, providing an opportunity to consider their needed resources, skill set, and who they are as a person when moving toward the accomplishment of said goals. Considerations should be made for the levels of motivation needed to accomplish goals as they transform, recognizing that they will not be equitable. Professionals also have to consider the importance of celebrating the successes-in-between that help allow for their intrinsic motivation to persist as they continue toward their primary long-term goal(s).

Case Example:

Marquita is a fourth-year doctoral student at *Very Expensive University*. She's spent that last year considering what type of work environment would be the best fit for her as a professional. Her choices are working in a university counseling center setting or starting a group practice with her friends. After taking some time to consider her past training experiences, planning for her time in internship in the year to come, and considering her immediate and future needs, she's decided to work with her friends to start a group practice. In order to accomplish their goal (open a group practice), there are lots of steps in between that can often feel daunting. In order to prevent burnout, disparagement, and undue stress, she and her friends set up a series of short- and long-term goals that would allow them to visualize their plan and find ways to celebrate as they move along.

Some of their long-term goals, and the short-term goals needed to accomplish them, included:

Choosing a practice name

- Brainstorm names in the shared Google Doc sheet
- Everyone add one name option a week for four weeks

Deciding what type of practice they'll own

- Develop a business plan
- Decide what type of clients to see
- Find insurance companies to panel and credential through
- Decide between an LLC, LTD, or Inc.

Setting up their marketing materials

- Developing their website
- Setting up their social media
- Business cards and other handouts
- Logo design

Choosing a location

- Type of building
- City and neighborhood
- Consider access through public and private transportation

Opening the practice doors

- Decorating and furnishing
- Practice logistics

  - Scheduling and billing system
  - Phone and email
  - Etc.

- Seeing clients

Finishing touches

- Sending thank you cards to those that helped them along the way
- Time for self and group appreciation
- Naps and nosh

Marquita and her friends set up a system that allowed them to reward themselves each time a goal was met (short- or long-term). Short-term goal rewards included going out to dinner, going to the movies, and trips to museums and festivals. Long-term goal rewards included group vacations and concerts. The initial value of having their own practice where they would have complete autonomy over how it functions, whom they serve in the community, and their own personal/professional development was key. They considered their available resources (startup capital, mentors, access to consultants, etc.) and recognized that the likelihood that they'd fail would be low, though they recognized that putting a time limit on when everything would be completed would cause too much strain. An open-ended approach to opening the doors to their practice allowed them to work toward their goals without the fear of missing a deadline. All of these considerations kept them highly motivated at their core, and the value of that motivation was readily increased when given opportunities to celebrate their big and successes-in-between.

"Expectancy-value theories hold that people are goal-oriented beings. The behaviors they perform in response to their beliefs and values are undertaken to achieve some end" (Palmgreen, 1984). Marquita and her friends' behaviors were directly influenced by the value placed on the work they hoped to do as clinicians, their beliefs about who they are as professionals, their perceived capabilities, as well as the underlining psychosocial drive towards self-actualization that allowed for the continual promotion of professional autonomy and its required motivation needed to obtain the desired work-product. This sense of self is tantamount to your potential success moving forward.

Continually place yourself in the position to consider your worth. That worth-value will be the foundation that regularly motivates you toward the completion of your goals regardless of the amount of time it takes, or pitfalls you stumble upon. It will reinvigorate your faith in your ability to persist, and provide you with a level of resilience that can be drawn upon during times of doubt.

Social Media

Get comfortable with the importance of social media and brand recognition. Past emphasis was placed on newspaper/magazine ads, commercials on television, and emails; while we don't want you to forget about the more vintage ways of marketing as they're still important, newer forms of information disbursement have shown to increase your visibility and brand recognition. Apps and sites such as Snapchat, Instagram, Facebook, YouTube, Twitch, and Twitter have millions of followers that are continually looking to engage in the world around them. Use this knowledge to think creatively about various ways to connect with others.

What to Do

- Develop a streamlined ad that has your business name, best method of contact, a brief snapshot of the service(s) you provide, and where you're located.
- Reach out to popular pages whose audiences mirror your target treatment population and request their ad posting price, and how long your ad will be available on their page.
- Develop and save a series of hashtags that you can simply copy and paste when you post to your own accounts that will increase traffic to your pages. This keeps you from having to remember them all, and risk forgetting one.
- Get in the habit of posting regularly to your business's social media pages. Review the analytics of your pages to see when your posts get the most views so you know when is the best time to post.
- Keep things interesting by adding pictures, colorful text, and/or the usage of memes in order to grab the attention of readers who scroll quickly looking for something unique to divert more of their attention toward.
- Respond to as many of your direct messages as possible, and like comments when appropriate.
- Develop relationships with influencers and social media users with similar focuses as yours in order to regularly cross-promote your services.
- Get a social media manager if you don't have the time or ability to manage your accounts on your own.

What Not to Do

- Ignore your followers and potential followers. There's no need to respond to every comment, but regularly engaging with those reaching out to you helps continue to build the relationship between both of you allowing for added visibility and a healthier reputation within the community.
- Don't be defensive. Taking pride in your work is essential, yet you should be mindful that not everyone will see the value in your work in the same way that you do, and some may at times meet you with adversity. Find neutral ways of dealing with negative feedback and responses, and don't feed into attempts at trolling.
- No "ghosting." Be sure to post regularly. Not doing so risks your followers forgetting about you.
- Watch out for homogeneity in content. Make your posts diverse in presentation (videos, quotes, polls, pictures, etc.) while championing the same message.
- Don't plagiarize. You lose nothing by tagging/crediting the original source of your content. However, you may lose your integrity as a brand if

you regularly take the work capital of others in an attempt to pass it off as your own.

Social media in all of its forms can be intimidating, but it's your best ally in a world that prioritizes a need for continual connection. If you're having trouble understanding the ins and outs of the various platforms, start by setting up your own personal accounts and play around with the various types of posting options. Audit how well your posts do based on time of day, type of post (video, picture, quote, etc.), whether you're getting "likes" and comments, and what type of feedback you're receiving about your content. Keep in mind that when setting up a business page on most social media platforms, it will provide you with a set of metrics that allow you to better understand your posts and the activity associated with them.

Marketing

"No one wants to buy counseling," says therapy branding expert Casey Truffo. "They search for answers to problems they have" (The Wellness Institute, 2019). With this in mind, it's imperative that mental health professionals understand the importance of marketing as a function of brand development. Marketing provides the space necessary to openly disclose your goals, values, services, and the measure of your previous accomplishments. Without comprehensive marketing strategies, aimed toward the communities the practitioner wishes to serve, the foundation of brand development falls short. As mentioned previously, marketing options have evolved over the years, and practitioners should honor those changes while still using historical methods that fit their needs. Below are a few considerations to keep in mind when thinking about the type of marketing materials that will work best for your brand.

Tangibles

Consider previous dialogue related to the one-panel rack card created for Coffee Hour, and the ways in which color choice, image selection, and simple yet direct statements about the organization make it appealing to pick up and captivating enough to hold on to for further consideration. A tangible is anything you can put in a potential consumer's hand that will help them remember you. Find what feels authentic to you in your design concepts, and work to keep the central theme recognizable when developing your various marketing tools. Some of those tangibles include the following:

- business cards
- table cloths

- rack cards
- pamphlets
- stickers
- flyers
- cards and invitations
- letterheads
- menus
- postcards

Website

A website is an opportunity for you to showcase your values, services, staff, and other desired pieces of information to a global audience with just one click. Website traffic can work hand in hand with email marketing. "According to the Washington Post, the average person spends 4.1 hours every single day on their email account. That adds up to more than 20 hours weekly. Even 79% of people say that they check their *work email* on vacations" (Patel, 2018). Using email marketing in order to drive traffic to your website will increase your service utilization, and provides a one-stop-shop for consumers and potential consumers to get better acquainted with you and your brand.

Be mindful of the chosen domain name, as it should be synonymous with your business name. Also, the layout should highlight what's most important for your business on the first page, and you want your site to be user friendly and intuitive. This means there should be no guess work on how to navigate the website in order to find contact information, a services menu, information about the staff, event information, and other pertinent data. Keep the site uncluttered so as not to overwhelm potential consumers, make the design thoughtful and memorable, and don't hesitate to consult with others about the utility of the site itself. To take things a step further, one should consider allowing consumers the ability to sign up for and pay for services by adding a space to the site where consumers can take care of these matters with little to no issue.

The About page of the Changing Perspectives website gives a brief overview of the practice, has a clean background that allows the photo and logo to stand out, and the top right legend allows for ease in navigation.

The "Who We Are" Page provides a photo of all team members along with brief staff biographies allowing consumers and colleagues to grasp whom they may be working with and who is responsible for particular services throughout the practice.

The "Services" page provides detailed information on what is offered through the practice, with the main services highlighted for ease in selection, along with detailed information about those services. The price points aren't provided as things may change subject to insurance, pro-bono availability, sliding scale, and other factors.

Word of Mouth

Letting others speak for you through their own experiences adds an interpersonal connection to your professional identity that's unmatched. This is where your reputation will proceed you; so whatever you do, be the most authentic version of yourself so that when your story is told, it's as accurate as possible.

Elevator Speech

The 15- to 30-second pitch about your brand sums up your values, goals, mission, and how your product is delivered. Get in the habit of practicing them, tailoring them to various environments and populations, and having a "tangible" in had to present to the person with whom you're speaking. For example, "Coffee Hour is a space for mental health professionals of colors to grow professionally and personally. We often don't have the same flexibility, or permission even, to have our needs met holistically as professionals, and this organization gives us an opportunity to do that without also feeling the need to defend ourselves against larger systemic issues that often create barriers for us."

Networking

Learn about others and their brand(s) as they learn about yours through systemic means of developing interpersonal relationships that will assist in the career pursuits, business advancements, and personal development of all involved. Networking can happen in-person (conferences, chance meetings, workshops, school, the grocery store, etc.) or online (via engagement on social media, emails, blogs, etc.). As a reminder, this is where you use your *elevator speech*, and your *tangibles*.

A comprehensive marketing strategy is the glue that binds the work that's done, with the goals for the community held at the center of the services offered. The key to quality marketing practices is to have clarity in your mission, be settled in your values, and to be open to various forms of connecting with others. As the landscape of therapeutic practice and psychological services grows and shifts, it is important that we as providers offer opportunities to cultivate innovative strategies related to consumer engagement, foster a healthy multiculturally competent environment that prioritizes the various ways individuals seek out and gather information, and partner regularly with other providers and consultants to cross-promote services in order to increase visibility, community outreach efforts, and promote the importance of psychological services.

KNOW YOUR WORTH

Most mental health and helping professionals do their jobs because they altruistically want to help others in their pursuit to become a better version of themselves. In service of that drive, the needs of these professionals often go unmet, and the necessary hygiene factors, specifically salary, associated with their labor are not achieved. When considering salary needs, a future practitioner should research current market trends associated with their field of choice (paying attention to specialization distinctions), ask human resource managers about the salary range of the position you're interested in for the last three people that held that position, and more importantly, get comfortable talking about how much money you make and asking others to be direct and candid about their salaries as well. Otherwise, you'll never truly know if you're being paid a fair market price if you are unable to get over the discomfort of discussing finances. This open dialogue prevents organizations from underselling you when offering you a salary, and you can ensure that issues of bias aren't impacting what you're offered versus others.

Negotiating your salary is essential, and the process starts at the application. Most applications now ask you for your current and your expected salary. When confronting the question of your expected salary, your best course of action is to write in "Negotiable," leave it blank if possible, or submit the number "00000" when required to enter a dollar amount. This prevents employers from offering you less when considering your application. When asked during the interview if you have any salary requirements, be sure to state that your salary requirements are negotiable. Follow this by asking what the proposed salary range for the position is, as well as any benefits packages, signing bonuses, and added covered expenses (travel, lodging, tuition reimbursement, professional development funds, gym membership, child-care, etc.). Until you have an understanding about their intent to offer, it is your best course of action to remain in the position of withholding your specified salary minimum.

Once an offer is made, check in about their proposed salary, and inquire how long you can hold your offer before making a final decision. This gives you time to process the offer holistically considering what makes it a good and poor fit. It also gives you time to consider how the salary may impact your day-to-day life and desired financial goals. Once you're ready to return to the offer, ask if the salary is negotiable a final time, and if so, ask them what their best offer is. Once a best offer is received, go back with a counteroffer that's slightly higher than the one previously mentioned. For the right candidate, companies with the necessary financial resources will happily accept your offer.

Some companies (small group practices, small not-for-profits, and other small businesses) don't have the same flexibility, and that should be considered when negotiating. Continue to follow the guidelines as discussed, but be prepared for their offer to be a set rate.

Keep in mind that this isn't solely about salaried positions. The same principles can be applied to contractual work, hourly work, and other fee-for-service employment opportunities. For instance, when setting the pricing structure for your private practice, consult with other private practice employees and owners to determine whether you're setting yourself below the industry standard, and if you're above, this is a chance to determine whether or not you may be pricing yourself out beyond the competition. In order to ensure uniformity in your pricing, set a pricing structure list that you can use as a guide when making these negotiations. Also, complete a salary and job analysis annually to determine whether your rates are competitive and/or meet your desired outcomes.

Example: Consultation services through Changing Perspectives begin at $250 per hour, with a recommended two-hour initial appointment. This two-hour period focuses on better understanding the structure of the organization in need of support, the nature of the problem, an overview of the different options available to the consumer based on what's learned during this initial assessment, and the onset of plan development to begin resolving the presenting concern.

THE LOOK

What's considered professional is more fluid now more than it's ever been. While there are certain professions that stick to traditional means of physical presentation when representing the company and its culture, helping professionals often work in spaces where there's more flexibility. Consider the organization with which you work, and the culture as it relates to how homogenous its team members present. For instance, a college counseling center will not require you to wear a tailored suit to meet with students. However, they may have a business casual office attire mandate that they loosely follow. Even still, the business casual structure may also be reserved for special events that require the staff to meet with parents, the board of trustees, the provost, or other higher-level employees. Otherwise, jeans and a T-shirt may be the norm. Keep the culture and message you'd like to present in mind when thinking of your wardrobe for events you'll be attending as a representative of your brand, and how that may or may not impact the perceptions of others. Find balance between presenting your most authentic self in your dress, and what may be necessary for the environment you're in.

Hair color and tailoring may also be a point of contention depending on where you're employed. Be sure to check in with your employer about their standards related to hair styles, colors, and facial hair tailoring. However, when working through your own private practice, or business, be sure to consider what you feel is the best way to present yourself. Keep in mind, your potential clients and contractors may make inferences about your professionalism based on that appearance. Personal grooming is just that, personal. Calculated considerations of potential consequences (both positive and negative) are imperative when stepping out as your brand ambassador. Be comfortable in your choice, and steadfast in your identity.

It should go without saying, but it's necessary to do so, that people of color and members of certain marginalized groups continue to deal with issues of systemic oppression in the form of workplace and hiring discrimination solely on the basis of the richness of their melanin, visible religious dress, perceived sexuality, visible physical impairments, gender presentation, and age. Not only are these identity variables known to carry weight on their own, but their intersections can set some candidates further behind the starting line than their peers. This is why a truly diverse hiring staff, management team, and employee pool are essential for honoring the needs of potential salaried employees and independent contractors. "People can talk as much as they want about equity, but what they have to do is put in place the structures and policies that enable folks to function given that knowledge of the truth. Equity has to be figured into a pragmatic approach towards finding solutions to our problems" (DeGruy, 2018).

For instance, a bigoted contractor looking to hire a consultant to work with her business partners on examining their company culture may offer the opportunity to a less-qualified White, cis-male presenting, psychologist before they offer the position to a Sikh, brown skinned, cis-male psychologist. These biases will exist in most rooms you enter. This makes it even more important for you to continually work toward acceptance of who you are in all of your intersecting identities. In the end, your values, your look, work-product and effort reflect how you see yourself as a consummate professional, and how seriously you take your craft. Give yourself permission and time to hone in on your identity, and then work toward making it universal across the spectrum of your brand. When you're making choices about how you choose to dress, piercings, tattoos, your hair, business materials, and your chosen linguistics, you're doing so based on your push toward authenticity, not the persona you hope others will accept.

MENTORSHIP OR SUPERVISION?

Supervision is often characterized by being a task-oriented process that solely focuses on ensuring that a subordinate is keeping in line with policies and procedures as outlined by their specified role(s). Mentorship focuses more on developing a more intimate working relationship, where time can be spent on the deeper-level processes that inform the decisions made by a subordinate. Mentorship allows for adherence to quality measures, but can also focus more on inherent strengths and growth edges to build holistic support for the mentee. While there's flexibility within each construct to adhere to both troupes, mentors and supervisors alike have the ability to support trainees and early career professionals along the task of developing their brands and professional identity. This can be done through self-as-example measures (e.g., disclosing the conception and inner working of Coffee Hour to a mentee) where the mentor or supervisor pulls from past personal experiences to teach on how to overcome challenges within the field, and navigate specific focus areas. It can also be accomplished via encouraging the mentee or supervisee to research the history of those areas of focus coupled with innovative measures allowing for ease in execution in the present.

In all things, either relationship should be bound within the principles of providing a safe space for growth, ease in access to one another as outlined by time-honored boundaries established early on, comfort in disclosure, multiculturally competent modes of support, and thorough feedback that doesn't solely focus on ways in which improvements can be made. These are all important considerations as you transition into personal branding. Be prepared to ask questions surrounding the length of time you can expect to dedicate to establishing yourself; the logistics around securing licensures, titles, and so forth, and best practices on how to network as a function of brand development. What it means financially to embark on this journey and how to balance your day-to-day life with the expectations of business ownership are also important factors for consideration. While this is not an exhaustive list of areas to address with a seasoned professional, these are the basis by which early career professionals can orient initial dialogues that show true dedication to their own professional development. An experienced mental health professional can't properly provide guidance if their trainee is unwilling to be direct about the support needed. Be open, be honest, and be direct. Come prepared with an understanding that while you're there to be guided, it's also appropriate for the trainee to set expectations on what you wish to learn within this working relationship.

FINAL THOUGHTS

It can be intimidating to embark on the journey of entrepreneurship. Even if the goal isn't to solely work independently, the dedication required for successful brand development should never be minimized. The process can be better approached with tangible supports in the forms of supervisors, mentors, and personal support systems. These relationships will be essential in providing countless opportunities to maintain a sounding board for your ideas, and serve as the first buffer to the perception given off by your efforts. While a fresh and experienced perspective is imperative, don't discount the value in your own understanding of networking, marketing, and creative devices that provide you with a clear picture on who you are as a function of your business endeavors. In considering how you wish to present yourself to the world, keep in mind how you orient your values, your mission, and your expertise as these principles will guide you along your path toward actualizing your brand.

REFERENCES

DeGruy, J. (June 27, 2018). How to suppot Black students: An interview with Dr. Joy DeGruy. Retrieved from https://chalkboardproject.org/news/blog/how-support-black-students-interview-dr-joy-degruy

DeVries, H. (August 10, 2018). The greatest business branding strategy in the world. Retrieved from https://www.forbes.com/sites/henrydevries/2018/08/10/the-greatest-business-branding-strategy-in-the-world/#3ad36d145512

Fishbein, M., & Ajzen, I. (1975). *Belief, attitude, intention, and behavior: An introduction to theory and research.* Reading, MA: Addison-Wesley.

Palmgreen, P. (1984). Uses and gratifications: A theoretical perspective. In R. N. Bostrom (Ed.), *Communication Yearbook 8* (61–72). Beverly Hills, CA: Sage Publications.

Patel, Neil. (2018). 4 old-school marketing tactics making a comeback in 2018. [Web log comment]. Retrieved from https://neilpatel.com/blog/old-school-marketing-tactics/

Wellness Institute. (2019). Web guide: Marketing for therapists. Retrieved from https://www.wellness-institute.org/marketing-for-therapists

Chapter Seven

Pedagogy of Wokeness

A Conceptualization of Black Millennial Liberation

Jacquelin Darby

Within the last five years, there has been an increase in the demand for social justice among the younger Black American generation. For example, in 2008 Black Millennials had the highest Black voting rates in America (Taylor & Lopez, 2013). Millennials are advocating for social change by engaging with others on a larger scale. Black Millennials are moving past the traditional ways of social engagement (e.g., voting, garnering signatures) and are finding ways to raise awareness of Black social issues outside of their own culture. The social engagement is not solely about stimulating change, but it is also a way to remind people of their humanity. This is done with the use of technology, art, and with the internet. Millennials are using creative means to express themselves and to shape their own narrative regarding liberation. As clinicians, it is important to understand the current movement and to attempt to conceptualize the rise in liberation within this Black generation. In doing so we can develop ways to help individuals to cope with the stressors of liberation. The goal of this chapter is to provide a framework for clinicians to conceptualize, highlight the role of social media, and provide recommendations for providers to support individuals who are becoming more liberated in this new civil rights movement.

Paulo Freire's model of liberation uses education as a tool for social liberation. Although the model has roots in Liberation Psychology, Freire's model differs in the method that is used to gain liberation. Freire argues that oppression comes once humanity of those oppressed is no longer recognized (Freire, 1996). The use of technology has impacted the ways in which individuals view humanity. On one hand, technology can showcase the stories of others thus reminding people of the humanity that lost, and on the other hand can give a voice to individuals who have been silenced (Mina, 2019). Technology can spread awareness of the struggles that individuals face which can build empathy toward others. Technology can also limit the presence of humanity by reducing individuals to an object that is in void. Individuals often feel emboldened to attack others when the person is just represented by an avatar. This can be seen with the recent uptick of racial and violent bullying that is taking place on popular social media sites. It is hard to get others to view your humanity when the device that enables that process is also allowing for attacks to happen. Black Millennials are often on the end of those attacks and are left with no ways to defend themselves without facing some repercussions themselves. Several social media advocates tell stories about them being locked out of their account for pointing out the injustices.

Freire contends that it is the job of the oppressed individual to remind the oppressor of their humanity—in doing so freeing the group of the oppressors from a script of othering. The war of liberation is fought from two fronts; from the side of the oppressed and from the side of the oppressor. Freire believed that the best way to remove the script of othering was to start with giving the younger generation the opportunity to format their own script through a choice of education. Education is often a tool used by the oppressed individuals to indoctrinate the next generation. The act of liberation serves as an "awakening" of not only the oppressed culture by reminding them of the cultural identity, but it is an awakening for the oppressor to see the other beings as humans and not as things meaning to be conquered.

Currently, there is an awakening within the Black Millennial culture. This awakening is done not just through formal education but by the use of technology and social media. Thanks to the internet, individuals have access to a wealth of information and culture that was once hidden from parts of the world. Social media has allowed for others to create their own narrative to shape what is shown to the outside world. It has also allowed for the creating of a "co-presence" with others because the line between physical and digital is being opaque (Mina, 2019). The blending of the worlds has allowed others to see the shared identities of each other and thus breaking the scripts of oppression.

With the increased accessibility of the internet more individuals have access to an education that is inclusive. Educational advocates are encouraging an educational system that features various cultural histories as well as giving students access to the knowledge at a young age. No longer are young Black students made to wait until college to receive education on African American history. That information is taught at younger ages with some schools forming an educational curriculum specifically focused on ethnic and racial identity. Studies have found that increased awareness of Black history has led to an increase in self-esteem, greater identity development, and resilience against racist bias (Chapman-Hilliard & Adams-Bass, 2016). This resilience is needed as Black Millennials are continuing the torch carried by others during the Civil Rights Movement. The access to Black history is helpful as Black Millennials discover ways to unlearn their own "othering scripts" that they have formed within their own communities.

The practice of incorporating "culturally relevant" information into institutions has been increasing over time. Companies and institutions are quickly trying to create "safe spaces" and "inclusive practices" and have made it a priority to have more individuals of the oppressed communities in the areas where they can implement change. However, Black Millennials are recognizing that it is not just enough to offer these inclusive policies to pacify the oppressed individuals; they are demanding that these oppressed communities are heard. This demand has been made not just by the use of traditional civil rights protest. This demand has moved past voting and boycotting, but rather it has expanded into Black Millennials taking up spaces in places where they can be at the forefront of the decision-making process. This demand can be seen in the election of "nontraditional" political leaders that have been elected into office. Black Millennial's journey to liberation is unique because they have moved from getting the oppressor to see their humanity to demanding that the oppressors respect their humanity.

Black Millennials are working hard to distinguish the ways in which their messages are being heard. Black Millennials have moved from taking a passive approach to more direct approaches to fighting injustices. Black Millennials are using creative measures to express themselves in ways that are getting noticed by the world and in doing so they are spreading the message of liberation. They are using memes, viral blog posts, and sharing music to advance the cause. Examples of this phenomenon can be seen in the use of popular internet sayings such as "We are not our grandparents." This message can be tracked by social users which can make it easier for individuals to add to the story. Black Millennials are using multiple ways to spread the narrative of their resistance. Black Millennials are being more intentional in selecting which platform where the message will be displayed. Black Millennials are questioning the status quo of the way that the media is handling their message. Black Millennials have taken a step past Freire's idea of liberation because they are not just shaping what information they are receiving, but they are shaping how information is being shared.

Appealing to the oppressors by using social media is not just limited to the viral sayings but is also done by highlighting the incidents of racism that occur in America. Prior to the widespread access to the internet, stories of racism were passed down from generation to generation like a folktale. It was often easy to hide and dismiss because the "proof" was easily restricted to just the Black culture. Domestic attacks were often treated like folklore within the Black community, passed down from one generation to the next generation. Often, the retelling of these attacks are left out of the overall American narrative. Black Millennials' use of social media make it difficult for the oppressors to deny the mistreatment of Black people because they are expanding the folklore. They are using visual evidence and the viral culture to show what is often kept in the dark. It is hard to hide one's racist thoughts when everything is just a screenshot away from going viral. Black Millennials are holding the group of oppressors accountable even when the law does not. There have been countless stories of individuals who have lost their jobs (i.e., Rosanne Barr, CEO of Papa Johns), privacy ("Permit Patty"), and scholarship because of social media. Social media allows for other individuals to assist with holding others accountable. It does not take time for others to identify the name, place of employment, school, and other identifying information. Not only are Black Millennials holding the perpetrators accountable, but they are also holding the employers accountable.

By holding individuals accountable for their racist actions, Black Millennials are not just affecting the oppressors they are stirring the idea of liberation in the oppressed individuals. Black Millennials are showing others that perpetrators can be held accountable and no longer should acts of injustice be hidden in folklore. It is stroking the fires of righteous indignation in hopes that people will rally behind a cause. This has been by the use of the hashtag #HandsUpDon'tShoot, the spreading of information that acknowledges acts of political actions, or by honoring victims of a police brutality via a hashtag. These acts keeps the oppressive action in the forefront of the collective unconscious and serves as a reminder that the fight for justice is still strong.

The use of social media provides proof to all that the United States is not as "progressive" as the media portray it. The FBI reported that in 2018 the number of incidences of personal attacks that were motivated by bias reached a sixteen-year high. Although attacks on property were down, attacks against people were up and made up around 61 percent of the reported cases (Hassan, 2019). The factors that led to the increase can vary; however, it would be hard to assume that the current sociopolitical climate did not have some influence on the numbers. The climate could have led to an increase in people feeling emboldened to commit these acts; however, it could have also led to people feeling more confident in reporting these acts. It is unclear, nevertheless, that the United States is not as progressive as others may have wished for it to be.

The realization that the country is not as "post-racial" may force individuals out of the pre-encounter phase of their racial identity to the encounter stage of development (Cross, 1971). In 1971 Dr. William Cross created a model that attempted to define phases that Black-identified individuals move through as they begin to understand their racial identity. The stages are pre-encounter, encounter, immersion/emersion, internalization, internalization-commitment. This model has been revised and critiqued by several scholars, yet the first phase is always the same and that is the pre-encounter phase.

This phase was first described as individuals having a "pro-White" mentality. Individuals within this phase were not consciously uplifting Whiteness, but rather they were attributing overly positive things to Whiteness while not recognizing their own race (Cross, 1995). They seek acceptance within the White culture at the cost of not acknowledging their own culture. Social media thrusts individuals into the encounter stage by promoting images and stories that showcase that the White culture in which they seek to assimilate into is not as welcoming as they would have hoped. They are thrust into a confusing time in which they realize that their race is a factor. The process of entering the Cross's encounter stage of identity development is similar to Freire's desire to remove the oppressive scripts within society. Both phases require an awakening from a previous notion to a world in which they were not prepared to face. These images, memes, stories, and videos provide proof that their interpersonal script that "racism is in the past" is wrong. They are now forced to understand their own racial identity and the role that they play in the act of oppressing or being the oppressed. By using technology, Black Millennials are purposely forcing that shift in the cognition in both the oppressed and oppressor's mind because they are showing that oppression does not just happen "over there" but it can happen right in their backyard.

Social media has been a useful tool for Black Millennials to seek out liberation, but it has also been a way for individuals to block liberation. Those individuals who attempt to stop the rise of liberation do not only come from the side of the oppressors but from the side of the oppressed. Black Millennials have termed these individuals as "hoteps," which is a play on the Egyptian word meaning "at peace" and has come to describe an individual who is blinded by Afrocentric ideals that they are blocking the progress of the people in which they claim to love. It is used to shame those who claim "enlightenment" even though they are clearly working hard to grasp whatever little privilege that their oppressed state grants them. Damon Young from VerySmartBrothas (2018) best describes hoteps as "individuals who wish to replace White male patriarchy with Black male patriarchy," which is the one thing that Freire warns against in the fight for liberation. Freire encourages individuals to view liberation as an "all or nothing" concept. Liberation is not just granted to the select few but rather it should be granted for all. Freire encourages the people to help those who wish to crush their efforts see the benefit of inclusive liberation. The liberation movement that is being demonstrated through Black Millennials calls for the liberation of individuals across all communities, genders, and orientations. The desire for these individuals to replace White patriarchy with Black patriarchy is the unconscious activation of a defense against their own narcissistic need to be in power. For these Black Millennials it is unnerving to ask for freedom and liberation because if everyone has equity then how will they display their power? If they are no longer unique, then how will they separate themselves from others? The need to maintain status quo comes from their inability to form their own identity. Additionally, the practice of having selective liberation and behaving in this manner prevents "hoteps" from recognizing their own oppressive attitudes and behaviors that they have toward others. Their desire to limit liberation is an attempt to project all their negative attributes to the oppressor while maintaining the role as victim. Instead of understanding and dealing with that aspect of themselves, they suppress it and fight hard to maintain the status quo.

It is important for clinicians to understand this new push for liberation driven by Black Millennials. Research has shown that activists that are involved in these movements are experiencing higher amounts of mental health concerns (Jones-Eversley, Adedoyin, Robinson, & Moore, 2017). Studies have shown that individuals who are repeatedly shown videos of the daily violence toward Black individuals are reporting trauma-like symptoms (Williams, 2016). These responses are not surprising given that on a daily basis these individuals are being repeatedly exposed to videos of brutality, micro-aggressive behaviors, and unnecessary use of local police. While it is helpful for liberation that the use of media can lead to widespread awareness, the downside is that the internet does not create safe spaces where individuals can process their feelings (Williams, 2016). For these Black Millennials there is not a space in which they can escape, for when they try, they are harassed from others in doing so. Clinicians need to develop a mechanism that can serve these clients and provide a space for them to feel safe. This may require the willingness to go outside the norms of "traditional talk therapy." It may mean working with local religious leaders, community leaders, and teachers to develop a culturally appropriate treatment modality. It may mean having therapists at the marches or even providing services at lower fees. Furthermore, it may also involve a higher psychological presence on social media platforms. Whatever is developed must not just be a blanket statement of diversity to appease others. Similar to how Freire encouraged his students to take control of their education, clinicians need to allow for Black Millennials to take control of their healing. Having mental health providers study and understand the uniqueness of Black Millennials' fight for liberation can lead to an increase in support for individuals who are continuing the fight for liberation.

REFERENCES

Cross, W. E., Jr. (1971). The negro-to-Black conversion experience. *Black World*, 13–27.

Franklin, K. (1997). Psychosocial motivations of hate crime perpetrators: Implications from prevention and policy. Paper presented at a congressional briefing cosponsored by the American Psychological Association and the Society for the Psychological Study of Social Issues. Washington, DC.

Freire, P. (1996). Pedagogy of the oppressed. (M. B. Ramos, trans.) New York, NY: Penguin Books. (Original work published in 1970)

Hassan, A. (2019). Hate-crime violence hits 16-year high, F.B.I. reports. *The New York Times*. Retrieved from https://www.nytimes.com/2019/11/12/us/hate-crimes-fbi-report.html on December 18, 2019.

Jones-Eversley, S., Adedoyin, A. C., Robinson, M. A., & Moore, S. E. (2017). Protesting Black inequality: A commentary on the civil rights movement and black lives matter. *Journal of Community Practice, 25*(3), 309–324. doi: 10.1080/10705422.2017.1367343

Mina, A. X. (2019). *Memes to movements. How the world's most viral media is changing social protest and power*. Boston, MA: Beacon Press

Taylor, P., & Lopez, M. H. (2013). Six takeaways from the Census Bureau's voting report. Retrieved from http://journalism.berkeley.edu/conf/2014/immigration/wp-content/uploads/2014/04/TakeAwaysCensus-.pdf

Williams, M. (2016). White people don't understand the trauma of viral police-killing videos. *PBS News Hour*. Retrieved from https://www.pbs.org/newshour/nation/column-trauma-police-dont-post-videos on May 21, 2018

Young, D. (2018, February, 6) *What is a hotep? A very smart brother explains it all*. [Video File]. Retrieved from: https://www.facebook.com/verysmartbrothas/videos/10159849122495231/

Chapter Eight

The Civic Life of the Black Millennial

Candice C. Robinson

Millennials (born 1981–1997) (Frey, 2018) have been shaped by great societal triumphs as well as inequities through political, social, and economic changes. Like each generation before them, millennials have navigated a world that is vastly different from their parents, grandparents, and, for some, their siblings. Black Millennials in particular, which comprise 14 percent of the millennial population, have navigated an additional racialized experience (Frey, 2018; Allen, Davis, McDonald, & Robinson, 2020). As descendants of the Civil Rights Movement and Black Power Movement, Black Millennials grew up hearing stories of Jim Crow inequality as well as the backlash to the Civil Rights Legislation of the 1960s (e.g., Andrews, 1997; Bell, 2014; Bonilla-Silva, 2006; Hall, 2005; Morris, 1986; Reed, 2009; Robnett, 2000). Segregated communities, transportation, schools, and occupations, and all forms of systemic inequality were realities for their parents and grandparents. Mobilization through such organizations as Black Panther Party, Congress of Racial Equality (CORE), the National Association for the Advancement of Colored People (NAACP), National Urban League (NUL), Southern Christian Leadership Conference (SCLC), Student Nonviolent Coordinating Committee (SNCC), and individuals such as Ella Baker, Angela Davis, Dr. Martin Luther King, Jr., John Lewis, Huey P. Newton, Rosa Parks, A. Philip Randolph, Assata Shakur, Malcom X, and Whitney M. Young, Jr. were shared as legends. These groups and individuals' responses to challenging racial discrimination through disruptive tactics of marches and riots, working through political systems, activities of people who worked in the board rooms and through the systems, and organizational membership are considered legendary. As a result of the social movement activities of the generations before, Black Millennials were born into a new racial order (Bonilla-Silva, 2006, 2015; Parker 2016). The new racial order no longer is based in overt racism but includes discrimination through economic policies that disproportionately affect Black people, such as student loan debt, housing, and wealth (Brady, 2019; Hunter & Robinson, 2016; Jacobs & Dirlam, 2016; Parker, 2016; Rugh, Albright, & Massey, 2015). The reactions to the changing face of racial discrimination have had to be explicit. Black Millennials have made their voices known by any means necessary in response to the rapidly changing sociopolitical landscape of the United States over the last twenty years.

In this chapter, I argue that the world that Black Millennials live in is different than those of their ancestors and of their white counterparts. In order to effectively document their responses to these experiences, I observe the spectrum of activities that they engage in for social justice. Below, I recap several sociopolitical changes that have directly affected the experiences of this generation. I next discuss the spectrum in which people actively get involved in enacting social change. I then discuss examples of Black Millennials participating in social movement activities that are informed by a large ethnographic dataset that includes archival and newspaper digital sources, policy reports, popular media, blogs, interviews, and participant observation from January 2016 to August 2019 at National Urban League events. These activities range from volunteering, political participation, voting, and group membership to mobilizations, marches, protests, and riots. I conclude by discussing the importance of looking at generations at a variety of intersections through broad social movement communities. In order to portray the nuances of Black Millennial life, as well as their civic life, we cannot forget the variety of activities that they have already actively participated in, and led.

MAKE IT MAKE SENSE: SOCIAL AND POLITICAL CHANGE OF THE TWENTY-FIRST CENTURY

On face value, equality and upward mobility initially appeared to be attainable in the United States for millennials. Educational attainment rates, previously a marker for upward mobility, increased. As of 2015, 36 percent of this generation obtained a bachelor's degree or higher, with 23 percent of Black Millennials in particular having a bachelor's degree (Frey, 2018). In 2018, the total attainment of bachelor's degree by millennials rose to 39 percent (Bialik & Fry, 2019). Despite arguments at the turn of the twenty-first century stating that Americans were losing social capital, Millennials are the most connected generation through the technological advancements of social media sources such as Facebook, Twitter, and Instagram (Putnam, 1999; Zukin, Keeter, Andolina, Jenkins, & Carpini, 2006; Vogels, 2019).

On the other hand, the educational and technical gains have been cast in the shadow of crises. Following the post–World War II economic boom and the heightened racial justice activism of the 1960s and 1970s that was thought to be resolved, the United States is faced with unprecedented economic, social, and political challenges at the beginning of the twenty-first century (Killewald, Pfeffer, & Schachner, 2017; Parker, 2016; Piketty, 2015; Wodtke, 2016). The high level of education, for example, is shrouded by lack of appropriately funded jobs and rising student loan debt (Taylor, Fry et al., 2011). The average debt of a borrower that graduated in 2016 was $37,102, a 78 percent increase from ten years earlier (Chamber of Commerce, 2019). Those who graduated or came of age in 2008 faced the worst recession since the Great Depression (Killewald, Pfeffer, & Schachner, 2017; Kena et al., 2015; Piketty, 2015; Taylor, Parker et al., 2012). This introduction to the labor market being marred by slow opportunities has led to countless articles citing millennials as the reason that casual dining, homeownership, napkins, and other industries have begun to disappear (Taylor, 2018). Millennials were hit so hard during this time that as of 2016, 5.3 percent of the 16.6 percent of households in poverty are headed by a millennial—more than any other generation (Pew Research Center, 2017).

Black Millennials sit at the nexus of a generation without the upward mobility opportunities of previous generations and the increased attacks on Black people generally (Garcia & Stout, 2019; Tesler, 2016; United States Department of Justice, Federal Bureau of Investigation, 2018). While experiencing the negative effects of this generation, they are further impacted by their racialized status. Black Millennials experienced more inequality than their White counterparts. The average Black graduate in 2008 held $52,726 in debt as compared to their White counterparts' debt of $28,006 with trends leaning toward continued increase (Li & Scott-Clayton, 2016). Black Americans as a whole following the recession were more likely to be unemployed or underemployed. The average annual unemployment rate for Black workers in 2010 was 16 percent, compared to 8.7 percent for White people (Nunn, Parsons, & Shambaugh, 2019). Furthermore, the median wealth for Black Americans declined without fully recovering, putting Black people behind economically. This caused Black Millennials to be without the financial support of their families because of the lack of generational wealth (Wolff, 2018).

In addition to the economic stress, the political process was marked by controversy. The first presidential election that millennials could vote in was Texas Governor George W. Bush vs. Vice President Al Gore in 2000. That year saw a low turnout rate for people within the Millennial age demographic at that time, ages 18–24 with 36.1 percent of the vote (Jamieson, Shin, & Day, 2002). By 2008, the age group 18–24, entirely Millennial, had the highest turnout and helped to elect Barack Obama, the first Black President of the United States. Barack Obama ran on the platform of "change" in which his views on domestic public policy, including major health care reform and policies to reshape the economy, seemed to challenge the social order that had led to the recession. Obama was initially a beacon of hope. Unfortunately, his election changed something in American society that considered itself "post racial."

At the conclusion of his second term, there were countless examples of overt racial attacks to President Obama, increased voter suppression, mass incarceration, and racially motivated attacks to people of color by police officers and white people (Dyson, 2016; Guynn, 2018; King, 2018; Tribune Wire Reports, 2015). While dealing with the economic shock enacted on all Millennials, Black millennials were forced to face increased racial traumas. The first fifteen years of the new millennium included a whirlwind—rising student debt and income inequality, the first Black president, the backlash to a Black presidency, police brutality, and voter suppression—that have made Black Millennials learn to mobilize traditionally and extra-institutionally.

LET'S GET IN FORMATION: CIVIC LIFE OF BLACK MILLENNIALS

Black Millennials follow a trail of traditional civic life set for them by their ancestors. From the abolition movement to the Civil Rights Movement to the Black Power Movement and beyond, Black Americans have continuously been involved in activities that are dedicated to racial equality (Dagbovie, 2015; Minkoff, 1995; Morris, 1986, 2019; Robinson, 2019). These activities span from getting involved through organizing, writing, advocating, civic associations, individual volunteering, and mentoring to events more disruptive in nature such as boycotts, marches, protests, and riots. Although Black Americans are often characterized as not investing within their own communities, scholars have acknowledged how they are the ultimate participants in democracy through their community-building activities (Morris, 1986; Myrdal, 1944; Skocpol, Liazos, & Ganz, 2006). This particular dedication to a just society helped to begin the process of closing a variety of gaps through civil rights legislation and forward progress to parity in the second half of the twentieth century. Unfortunately, the twenty-first century has halted many of the gains that were previously received. The fights of previous generations have been picked up by Black Millennials.

Foregrounding the work of the Black Millennials is the understanding of broad collective behavior and social movement theory. Scholarship on collective behavior and social movements during the mid-twentieth century attempted to understand the emergence of social movements (Jenkins & Eckert, 1986; McCarthy & Zald, 1977; Moss & Snow, 2016). A social movement is understood as informal and formal groups coming together to challenge governing structures (Moss & Snow, 2016). With the focus on high-risk forms of activism, such as protests and marches, social movement scholarship presumes that social change mainly spurns out of protest activity, with little attention to the activities conducted prior. The lack of attention to the holistic view of activities had made it difficult to predict upticks in engagement.

At the dawn of the twenty-first century, scholarship attempted to rectify this gap through studying the sustention of movements and the consequences of protest moments when it appeared that mobilization had waned (Staggenborg 1988; Taylor, 1989). However, much of the scholarship still does not put all forms of activity in conversation with one another. This false dichotomy ignores the ability for every generation, every individual, to be involved with a multitude of activities. Furthermore, the racial neutrality of many of these concepts limits the imagination to understand Black communities in particular (Bracey, 2016; Robinson, 2019). As early as the nineteenth century, W. E. B. Du Bois (1899, 1903) cited the ways that the Black community had the capacity for mobilization to spawn social change through individuals, organizations, and values. In essence, Black Millennials have lived in the shadow of a racial justice social movement community. A social movement community sets the foundation to observe all aspects of social movement activity, the contentious and traditionally institutional parts, as well as individuals and organizations (Staggenborg, 1988). A social movement community argues that the community has one particular goal; a racial justice social movement community thus focuses on the goal of racial equality. With the backdrop of a history of violence to Black people in America and these particular moments throughout their lifetime, I note that Black Millennials are active in a racial justice social movement community through both civic engagement and traditional protest activity. As discussed above, Black millennials have encountered barriers to income and wealth making it more difficult to give money but give their time and talents; however, here I want to chronicle the activities they have conducted. Statements on shirts like "I am my ancestors wildest dreams" and "Dear Racism, I am not my grandparents, Sincerely, these hands," are joined with the social movement work through civic engagement and protest activities.

Civic Engagement Activity

Civic engagement is broadly defined as voluntary activity conducted by citizens in support of one's community and society (Putnam, 1999; Robinson, 2019; Skocpol and Fiorina, 2004). In order to operationalize this concept, scholars observe it through voting, political participation, volunteering, and group membership. Black Millennials build on the traditions of the people before them, while also stepping into the spaces that they have created for themselves. Group membership, voting, and political participation are all areas in which Black Millennials are vocal. Considering that Black Millennials are often involved in a racial justice social movement community, many of their activities focus on racial equality.

Recently voter identification laws have once again become a barrier to the right to vote despite access to voting being a win of the Civil Rights Movement. The increase of strict voter identification laws has negatively impacted the turnout of minorities in primaries and general elections. With the increase of obstacles to voting, democracy has begun to skew toward those on the political right, which negatively affects Black people (Hajnal, Lajevardi, & Nielson, 2017). Regardless, Black millennials have worked to combat voter suppression as well as increasing their own involvement in voting. Since 2004, movements that target Black people like Rock the Vote and #TurnOutforWhat with the assistance of artists such as P. Diddy and Lil Jon directly target young Black people go out to vote. Even Cardi B has regularly taken to her Instagram to voice the importance of getting involved in the political process wherever one is at. Voter turnout in Black youth for elections during a presidential year went from 32.4 percent (all Gen Xers) in 2004 to 52.3 percent in 2008 (all Millennials). The 52.3 percent outpaced white voter turnout among youth that was at 41.4 percent (Rogowski & Cohen, 2015). In the upward tick of voting as a form of involvement, Millennials, along with Gen Zers and Gen Xers, outvoted older generations in the 2016 presidential election. Millennials in particular comprised 26 percent of the total vote (File, 2014).

In 2014, 70.8 percent of Black youth agreed that participating in politics can make a difference, and they have backed this up by ensuring that they are in the political rooms (Rogowski & Cohen, 2015). Beyond a life course perspective that essentially requires millennials to ultimately replace the generation before, millennials have shown to serve as the youngest in their states. Some notable Black Millennial mayors include Aja Brown (Compton, CA), Marita Garrett (Wilkinsburg, PA), Tamara James (Dania Beach, FL), Chardae Jones (Braddock, PA), Svante Myrick (Ithaca, NY), Michael Tubbs (Stockton, CA), and Randall Woodfin (Birmingham, AL). In Pennsylvania, Austin Davis (PA 35th District) and Summer Lee (PA 34th District) are two Black Millennials who represent Western Pennsylvania in Pennsylvania State Legislature. Currently, two of the twenty-six millennials in Congress are Black women. Ilhan Omar (Minnesota 5th District) and Lauren Underwood (Illinois 4th District) are further notable in their own ways. Omar is the first Somali-American elected to Congress and one of the first Muslim-Americans to serve in the House, while Underwood is the youngest black woman elected to Congress

In addition to making a difference through participating in politics, Millennials find themselves active through voluntary organizations. Black Millennials build on the traditions of older Black voluntary organizational structures. The church, Black Greek Lettered Organizations (BGLOs), National Urban League (NUL), National Association for the Advancement of Colored People (NAACP), and Black professional organizations like National Association of Black Journalists (NABJ), National Society of Black Engineers (NSBE), National Black MBA Association (NBMBA), and Association of Black Psychologists (ABPsy) have been in existence for decades and in many cases for over a century; however, Black Millennials still find these groups relevant (IsabelHerrera, 2017; Jamilah, 2019; Allen, David, McDonald, & Robinson, 2020).

These organizations have a history of serving as a foundation for Black communities to mobilize and often serve as a for the racial justice social movement community. NAACP and NUL in particular have targeted younger generations with young professional targeted programming. NAACP annually brings people together for their Next Generation (NextGen) program, a twelve-month leadership development training program for young adults between the ages of 21 and 35 to receive comprehensive leadership and advocacy training to develop leadership competencies to become effective civil rights leaders ("NAACP | NAACP NEXT GENERATION," 2019). NUL developed the National Urban League Young Professionals (NULYP) in 1999 that now has nearly 10,000 members ages 21 to 40, with the majority being Millennials (National Urban League Young Professionals, 2019). Members of NULYP conduct thousands of hours of community service, advocacy, and civic engagement annually (National Urban League Young Professionals, 2019). Continuing to pay attention to the rise of millennials getting involved, this generation makes their voices known through the founding of their own organizations that have social justice leanings.

Notable Black Millennial organizations include the Black Swan Academy, Black Millennials 4 Flint, Leaders of a Beautiful Struggle, Black Millennial Political Convention, Black Youth Project 100 (BYP100), and Black Lives Matter. Each of these organizations has a dedication to assist the next generation as well as strengthening the community Black Millennials have among themselves. Black Swan Academy ensures that the work continues by empowering Black youth through civic leadership and engagement (Black Swan Academy, 2019). Black Millennials 4 Flint bridges environmental justice with racial justice to advocate against lead exposure for Black and Latino communities throughout the United States (Black Millennials 4 Flint, 2019). Leaders of a Beautiful Struggle (LBS) is a grassroots think-tank which has advanced the public policy interest of Black people, in Baltimore, through youth leadership development, political advocacy, and autonomous intellectual innovation since 2010 (Leaders of a Beautiful Struggle, 2019). Black

Millennial Political Convention includes on its committee millennials Dr. Wes Bellamy, City Councilman in Charlottesville, VA, and Jewell Jones, the youngest state representative in Michigan's 11th District and the youngest black lawmaker in the United States. The Black Millennial Political Convention is a "convening of Millennials of African descent from across the country and the diaspora to advance racial equity, increase black political power, and expand civic engagement." Their guiding principles are pipeline-planting seeds, policy-institute policies, and power to the people-elevating Our Power. Each of these principles ensures that they are working with one another for themselves and for the future ("Black Millennial Convention | Black Millennial Convention," 2019).

While Black Swan Academy, Black Millennials 4 Flint, Leaders of a Beautiful Struggle, and Black Millennial Political Convention are voluntary organizations primarily focused on institutional changes, BYP100 and Black Lives Matter are more similar to traditional social movement organizations in which they participate more actively in direct action organizing. BYP100 has been in existence since 2013; it is a "national, member-based organization of Black eighteen to thirty-five year old activists and organizers, dedicated to creating justice and freedom for all Black people. We do this through building a network focused on transformative leadership development, direct action organizing, advocacy, and political education using a Black queer feminist lens" (BYP100, 2019). Black Lives Matter was also founded in 2013. Alicia Garza, Patrisse Cullors, and Opal Tometi developed an organization that is dedicated to centering the leadership of women, queer, and trans people. Now, it is a global network, chapter based, member led, with a mission "to build local power and to intervene in violence inflicted on Black communities by the state and vigilantes" (Black Lives Matter, 2019). Notably, the organizational structures and activities of BYP100 and BLM emerged out of a need for high-risk activism following the increased attack on Black people in the 2010s.

High-Risk Activism

Millennials as a generation were no strangers to mobilization, with cues from mobilizations against the Iraq War, Occupy Wall Street, Women's March, and the recent March for Our Lives (Campbell, 2011; Skoczylas, 2016). For Black Millennials, mobilization has occurred with a particular focus on racial inequalities. In 2006, six Black boys in Jena, Louisiana, brutally beat a white student following the hanging of nooses on a tree on the campus of their school. After they were charged with murder, civil rights leaders came together to protest charges as one of the largest civil rights demonstrations of the twenty-first century (NPR Staff, 2011). In 2009, individuals protested and rioted in Oakland, California, following the death of Oscar Grant. Oscar

Grant was shot, murdered by the Bay Area Rapid Transit (BART) police on New Year's Day (McKinley, 2009).

As the 2010s began, Black Millennials were privy to deaths of Black people by police officers and white people. The deaths of Trayvon Martin (2012, Sanford, FL); Jordan Davis (2012, Jacksonville, FL), Michael Brown (2014, Ferguson, MO), Eric Garner (2014, New York City, NY), Tamir Rice (2014, Cleveland, OH), Walter Scott (2015, North Charleston, SC), Freddie Gray (2015, Baltimore, MD), Sandra Bland (2015, Hempstead, TX), and numerous unnamed victims inspired an increase in mobilization as their murderers were often acquitted. Some of the demonstrations included "Ferguson October" and "Baltimore Uprisings" as people took to the streets to protest the unjust system (Baltimore Uprising, 2019; Stewart, 2014). Organizations led by Millennials like BYP100 and Black Lives Matter assisted in sustaining the mobilization of groups.

Additionally, individuals were involved on the national scene. In 2015, Bree Newsome was arrested for taking down the Confederate battle flag displayed at the South Carolina State House. She removed it in protest following the massacre of nine black parishioners by a white supremacist at Emmanuel AME Zion Church in Charleston, South Carolina. In building on previous generations, she has cited her knowledge of the Civil Rights Movement and the messages she has received to ensure that she continues to fight for the opportunities that previous generations were denied (Dillahunt, 2019). National Football League (NFL) player, Colin Kaepernick, took a knee during the national anthem throughout the 2016–2017 NFL season to protest social injustice and racial brutality. This act ultimately blackballed him from the NFL, but he has become the face of sacrificing for injustice through Nike (Allen & Miles, 2020; Creswell, Draper, & Maheshwari, 2018; Peter, 2016; Schmidt, Frederick, Pegoraro, & Spencer, 2019).

In these activities, Black Millennials find themselves in racial social movement communities continuing the work that was set forth by generations prior while mobilizing more quickly because of their access to technology. The public aspects of their work and use of social media technologies through hashtags has made them targets (Ray, Brown, Fraistat, & Summers, 2017). #BlackLivesMatter, #SayHerName, and the use of various hashtags has represented both symbolic forms of resistance in cyberspace as well as on-the-ground mobilizations—mobilizations that are dedicated to not only challenging racial inequities, but inequities at all of their intersections (Brown, Ray, Summers, & Fraistat, 2017). Black Millennials build upon the tactics that they have heard from previous generations, but even more so acknowledging the race, classed, and gendered dynamics that further influence these movements.

WE GON' BE ALRIGHT: CONCLUSION

Throughout this chapter, I have discussed the sociopolitical context in which Black Millennials must adjust to life as a Black person in America as well as a millennial as well as their activities in response. Their life is shrouded in inequities based on their generational experiences as well as their racialized experiences within America. In the shadow of these experiences, Black Millennials have continued to have active civic lives among the spectrum of group membership, voting, volunteering, mobilization, and high-risk activist forms.

While they ensure that the stories are told through their own voices through social media and podcasts, this chapter begins to ensure that these stories will not be overlooked and that the lives of the people who helped ensure mobilization are also not forgotten. The amount and types of engagement of Black Millennials are endless. In addition to these forms of traditional racial justice social movement community activities as discussed above, they find themselves using such items as music, television, film, blogs, magazines, podcasts, newspapers, clothing, and websites to get their voices out. As seen through the eyes of Kendrick Lamar, Zendaya, Ryan Coogler, The Root, VerySmartBrothas, The Read, and more, Black Millennials see their civic life steeps in everyday forms of combating racial injustices in addition to taking to the streets. I encourage scholars and theorists to think more critically about the ways we observe and talk about getting involved within society, without limiting to any particular activities.

This chapter ensures that we remember the names of victims of police brutality and the organizations and individuals who fight for their memories. I want to end by ensuring that we also remember several of the names of those who have sacrificed their lives in this work so that they may not get lost to history: Ericka Garner, MarShawn McCarrel, Edward Crawford Jr., Danye Jones, Bassem Masri, Deandre Joshua, and Darren Seals.

REFERENCES

Allen, S. E. (2019). Doing Black Christianity: Reframing Black Church Scholarship. *Sociology Compass, 13*(10), e12731. doi.org/10.1111/soc4.12731

Allen, S. E., Davis, I. F., McDonald, M., & Robinson, C. C. (2020). The Case of Black Millennials. *Sociological Perspectives, 63*(3), 478–485. doi.org/10.1177/0731121420915202

Allen, S., & Miles, B. (2020). Unapologetic Blackness in Action: Embodied Resistance and Social Movement Scenes in Black Celebrity Activism. *Humanity & Society.* doi.org/10.1177/0160597620932886

Andrews, K. T. (1997). The Impacts of Social Movements on the Political Process: The Civil Rights Movement and Black Electoral Politics in Mississippi. *American Sociological Review, 62*(5), 800. doi.org/10.2307/2657361

Baltimore Uprising. (2019). Home · Preserve the Baltimore Uprising: Your Stories. Your Pictures. Your Stuff. Your History. Retrieved November 11, 2019, from https://baltimoreup rising2015.org/

Bell, J. M. (2014). *The Black Power Movement and American Social Work*. Columbia University Press.

Bialik, K., & Fry, R. (2019, February 14). How Millennials compare with prior generations. Retrieved November 8, 2019, from Pew Research Center's Social & Demographic Trends Project website: https://www.pewsocialtrends.org/essay/millennial-life-how-young-adultho od-today-compares-with-prior-generations/

Black Lives Matter. (2019). About. Retrieved November 11, 2019, from Black Lives Matter website: https://blacklivesmatter.com/about/

Black Millennial Convention. (2019). Black Millennial Convention | Black Millennial Convention. Retrieved November 10, 2019, from https://blackmillennialconvention.com/

Black Millennials 4 Flint. (2019). Black Millennials 4 Flint. Retrieved November 11, 2019, from https://www.blackmillennials4flint.org/

Black Swan Academy. (2019). The Black Swan Academy. Retrieved November 11, 2019, from https://blackswanacademy.org/

Bracey, G. E. (2016). Black Movements Need Black Theorizing: Exposing Implicit Whiteness in Political Process Theory. *Sociological Focus, 49*(1), 11–27. doi.org/10.1080/0038023 7.2015.1067569

Brady, D. (2019). Theories of the Causes of Poverty. *Annual Review of Sociology, 45*(1), 155–175. doi.org/10.1146/annurev-soc-073018-022550

Brown, M., Ray, R., Summers, E., & Fraistat, N. (2017). #SayHerName: A Case Study of Intersectional Social Media Activism. *Ethnic and Racial Studies, 40*(11), 1831–1846. doi.org/10.1080/01419870.2017.1334934

BYP100. (2019). Retrieved November 10, 2019, from BYP100 website: https://byp100.org/

Campbell, E. R. A. (2011). A Critique of the Occupy Movement from a Black Occupier. *The Black Scholar, 41*(4), 42–51. doi.org/10.5816/blackscholar.41.4.0042

Campbell, L. A., & Kaufman, R. L. (2006). Racial differences in household wealth: Beyond Black and White. *Research in Social Stratification and Mobility, 24*(2), 131–152. doi.org/ 10.1016/j.rssm.2005.06.001

Chamber of Commerce. (2019). US student loan debt statistics in 2019—What is the average student loan debt? | Chamber of Commerce. Retrieved November 10, 2019, from https:// www.chamberofcommerce.org/student-loan-statistics/

Cohen, C. J., Fowler, M., Medenica, V. E., & Rogowski, J. (2017). The "woke" generation? Millennial attitudes on race in the US. Retrieved from GenForward Survey website: http:// genforwardsurvey.com/assets/uploads/2017/10/GenForward-Oct-2017-Final-Report.pdf

Creswell, J., Draper, K., & Maheshwari, S. (2018, September 26). Nike Nearly Dropped Colin Kaepernick before Embracing Him. *The New York Times*. Retrieved from https:// www.nytimes.com/2018/09/26/sports/nike-colin-kaepernick.html

Dagbovie, P. G. (2015). *What is African American history?* John Wiley & Sons.

Dillahunt, A. A. (2019, July 2). From hashtag activist to street protester: An interview with Bree Newsome Bass – AAIHS. Retrieved November 11, 2019, from https://www.aaihs.org /black-organizing-today-an-interview-with-bree-newsome-bass/

Du Bois, W. E. B. (1899). The Philadelphia negro: A social study. Retrieved from https:// www.amazon.com/Philadelphia-Negro-Social-Study/dp/1164108719

Du Bois, W. E. B. (1903). *The Souls of Black Folk*.

Dyson, M. E. (2016). Whose president was he? Retrieved November 11, 2019, from POLITI-CO Magazine website: https://www.politico.com/magazine/story/2016/01/barack-obama -race-relations-213493

File, T. (2014). Young-Adult Voting: An Analysis of Presidential Elections, 1964–2012. 12.

Frey, W. H. (2018). The millennial generation: A demographic bridge to America's diverse future. Retrieved from https://www.brookings.edu/research/millennials/

Garcia, J. R., & Stout, C. T. (2019). Responding to Racial Resentment: How Racial Resentment Influences Legislative Behavior. *Political Research Quarterly*, doi.org/10.1177/106591291 9857826

Guynn, J. (2018, July 23). BBQ Becky, Permit Patty and why the Internet is shaming white people who police people "simply for being black." Retrieved November 11, 2019, from USA TODAY website: http://www.usatoday.com/story/tech/2018/07/18/bbq-becky-permit -patty-and-why-internet-shaming-white-people-who-police-black-people/793574002/

Hajnal, Z., Lajevardi, N., & Nielson, L. (2017). Voter Identification Laws and the Suppression of Minority Votes. *The Journal of Politics, 79*(2), 363–379. doi.org/10.1086/688343

Hall, J. D. (2005). The Long Civil Rights Movement and the Political Uses of the Past. *Journal of American History, 91*(4), 1233–1263. doi.org/10.2307/3660172

Hunter, M. A., & Robinson, Z. F. (2016). The Sociology of Urban Black America. *Annual Review of Sociology, 42*(1), 385–405. doi.org/10.1146/annurev-soc-081715-074356

IsabelHerrera. (2017, December 5). 7 Minority professional organizations every millennial should know about tis' the season to step your network game up. Retrieved November 11, 2019, from Blavity News & Politics website: https://blavity.com/7-minority-professional -organizations

Jacobs, D., & Dirlam, J. C. (2016). Politics and Economic Stratification: Power Resources and Income Inequality in the United States. *American Journal of Sociology, 122*(2), 469–500. doi.org/10.1086/687744

Jamilah, G. (2019, March 5). 22 Events Black Professionals Should Attend This Summer. Retrieved November 11, 2019, from I DON'T DO CLUBS® website: https://idontdoclubs .biz/2019/03/05/best-black-summer-events-2019/

Jenkins, J. C., & Eckert, C. M. (1986). Channeling Black Insurgency: Elite Patronage and Professional Social Movement Organizations in the Development of the Black Movement. *American Sociological Review, 51*(6), 812–829. doi.org/10.2307/2095369

Jones-Eversley, S., Adedoyin, A. C., Robinson, M. A., & Moore, S. E. (2017). Protesting Black Inequality: A Commentary on the Civil Rights Movement and Black Lives Matter. *Journal of Community Practice, 25*(3–4), 309–324. doi.org/10.1080/10705422.2017.1367343

Kena, G., Musu-Gillette, L., Robinson, J., Wang, X., Rathbun, A., Zhang, J., . . . Dunlop Velez, E. (2015). The condition of education 2015 (NCES 2015-144). Retrieved from U.S. Department of Education, National Center for Education Statistics website: http://nces.ed.gov /pubsearch

Killewald, A., Pfeffer, F. T., & Schachner, J. N. (2017). Wealth Inequality and Accumulation. *Annual Review of Sociology, 43*(1), 379–404. doi.org/10.1146/annurev-soc-060116-053331

King, S. (2018, April 17). Data shows police brutality in America is getting worse—2018 could be the most deadly in years. Retrieved November 11, 2019, from The Appeal website: https://theappeal.org/data-shows-police-brutality-in-america-is-getting-worse-2018-could-b e-the-most-deadly-in-years-90c9fa503580/

Leaders of a Beautiful Struggle. (2019). Baltimore's Grassroots Think-Tank. Retrieved November 11, 2019, from Leaders of a Beautiful Struggle website: https://lbsbaltimore.com /about-us/history/

Li, J., & Scott-Clayton, J. (2016, October 20). Black-white disparity in student loan debt more than triples after graduation. Retrieved November 10, 2019, from Brookings website: https://www.brookings.edu/research/black-white-disparity-in-student-loan-debt-more-than-t riples-after-graduation/

Looney, A., & Yannelis, C. (n.d.). Is High Student Loan Debt Always a Problem? 6.

McCarthy, J. D., & Zald, M. N. (1977). Resource Mobilization and Social Movements: A Partial Theory. *American Journal of Sociology, 82*(6), 1212–1241. doi.org/10.1086/226464

McKinley, J. (2009, January 9). In California, Protests after Man Dies at Hands of Transit Police: [National Desk]. *New York Times*, Late Edition (East Coast); New York, N.Y., p. A.10.

Minkoff, D. C. (1995). *Organizing for equality: The evolution of women's and racial-ethnic organizations in America, 1955–1985.* Rutgers University Press.

Morris, A. (2019). Social movement theory: Lessons from the sociology of W. E. B. Du Bois. *Mobilization: An International Quarterly, 24*(2), 125–136. doi.org/10.17813/1086-671X-24 -2-125

Morris, A. D. (1986). *The Origins of the Civil Rights Movement.* Simon and Schuster.

Moss, D. M., & Snow, D. A. (2016). Theorizing Social Movements. In *Handbooks of Sociology and Social Research. Handbook of Contemporary Sociological Theory* (pp. 547–569). doi.org/10.1007/978-3-319-32250-6_26

Myrdal, G. (1944). An American dilemma: The negro problem and modern democracy. New York: Harper and Brothers.

NAACP | NAACP NEXT GENERATION. (2019). Retrieved November 10, 2019, from NAACP website: https://www.naacp.org/campaigns/naacp-next-generation/

National Urban League Young Professionals. (2019). National Urban League Young Professionals Annual Report.

Neckerman, K. M., & Torche, F. (2007). Inequality: Causes and Consequences. *Annual Review of Sociology, 33*(1), 335–357. doi.org/10.1146/annurev.soc.33.040406.131755

NPR Staff. (2011, August 20). Race, violence . . . justice? Looking back at Jena 6. Retrieved November 11, 2019, from NPR.org website: https://www.npr.org/2011/08/30/140058680/race-violence-justice-looking-back-at-jena-6

Nunn, R., Parsons, J., & Shambaugh, J. (2019, August 1). Race and underemployment in the US labor market. Retrieved November 10, 2019, from Brookings website: https://www.brookings.edu/blog/up-front/2019/08/01/race-and-underemployment-in-the-u-s-labor-market/

Oliver, M. L., & Shapiro, T. M. (2006). *Black Wealth, White Wealth: A New Perspective on Racial Inequality.* Taylor & Francis.

Parker, C. S. (2016). Race and Politics in the Age of Obama. *Annual Review of Sociology, 42*(1), 217–230. doi.org/10.1146/annurev-soc-081715-074246

Peter, J. (2016, September 1). Colin Kaepernick: I'm not anti-American, will donate $1 million. Retrieved November 11, 2019, from USA TODAY website: https://www.usatoday.com/story/sports/nfl/49ers/2016/09/01/colin-kaepernick-national-anthem-protest-police-socks/89743344/

Pew Research Center. (2017). More households headed by a Millennial are in poverty than other generations. Retrieved November 10, 2019, from Pew Research Center website: https://www.pewresearch.org/fact-tank/2017/09/06/5-facts-about-millennial-households/ft_17-09-05_millennialhouseholds_poverty/

Piketty, T. (2015). About "Capital in the Twenty-First Century." *The American Economic Review, 105*(5), 48–53.

Putnam, R. D. (1999). *Bowling Alone: America's Declining Social Capital.* New York: Palgrave Macmillan.

Ray, R., Brown, M., Fraistat, N., & Summers, E. (2017). Ferguson and the death of Michael Brown on Twitter: #BlackLivesMatter, #TCOT, and the evolution of collective identities. *Ethnic and Racial Studies, 40*(11), 1797–1813. doi.org/10.1080/01419870.2017.1335422

Reed, T. F. (2009). *Not Alms but Opportunity: The Urban League and the Politics of Racial Uplift, 1910–1950.* University of North Carolina Press.

Robinson, C. C. (2019). (Re)theorizing civic engagement: Foundations for Black Americans civic engagement theory. *Sociology Compass, 13*(9), e12728. doi.org/10.1111/soc4.12728

Robnett, B. (1996). African-American Women in the Civil Rights Movement, 1954-1965: Gender, Leadership, and Micromobilization. *American Journal of Sociology, 101*(6), 1661–1693. doi.org/10.1086/230870

Robnett, B. (2000). *How Long? How Long?: African-American Women in the Struggle for Civil Rights.* Oxford University Press.

Rogowski, J. C., & Cohen, C. J. (2015). Black Millennials in America. Black Youth Project.

Rugh, J. S., Albright, L., & Massey, D. S. (2015). Race, Space, and Cumulative Disadvantage: A Case Study of the Subprime Lending Collapse. *Social Problems, 62*(2), 186–218. doi.org/10.1093/socpro/spv002

Schmidt, S. H., Frederick, E. L., Pegoraro, A., & Spencer, T. C. (2019). An Analysis of Colin Kaepernick, Megan Rapinoe, and the National Anthem Protests. *Communication & Sport, 7*(5), 653–677. doi.org/10.1177/2167479518793625

Skocpol, T., & Fiorina, M. P. (2004). *Civic Engagement in American Democracy.* Brookings Institution Press.

Skocpol, T., Liazos, A., & Ganz, M. (2006). *What a Mighty Power We Can Be: African American Fraternal Groups and the Struggle for Racial Equality*. Princeton University Press.

Skoczylas, M. (2016, June 15). ANARCHISM AND PREFIGURATIVE POLITICS IN THE OCCUPY MOVEMENT: A STUDY OF OCCUPIED SPACE, HORIZONTAL STRUC-TURE, AND ANARCHIST THEORY IN PRACTICE [PhD diss. University of Pittsburgh ETD]. Retrieved November 10, 2019, from http://d-scholarship.pitt.edu/27602/

Staggenborg, S. (1998). Social Movement Communities and Cycles of Protest: The Emergence and Maintenance of a Local Women's Movement. *Social Problems, 45*(2).

Stewart, M. (2014, October 11). Ferguson October is here. Retrieved November 11, 2019, from HuffPost website: https://www.huffpost.com/entry/ferguson-october-protesters-streets_n _5971106

Taylor, K. (2018). Millennials and their spending habits are wreaking havoc on these 18 industries. Retrieved November 10, 2019, from Business Insider website: https://www.businessinsider.com/millennials-hurt-industries-sales-2018-10

Taylor, P., Fry, R., Cohn, D., Livingston, G., Kochhar, R., Motel, S., & Patten, E. (2011). The rising age gap in economic well-being. Retrieved from https://www.pewsocialtrends.org /2011/11/07/the-rising-age-gap-in-economic-well-being/

Taylor, P., Parker, K., Kochhar, R., Fry, R., Funk, C., Patten, E., & Motel, S. (2012). Young, underemployed and optimistic: Coming of age, slowly, in a tough economy. Retrieved from http://www.pewsocialtrends.org

Taylor, V. (1989). Social Movement Continuity: The Women's Movement in Abeyance. *American Sociological Review, 54*(5), 761–775. doi.org/10.2307/2117752

Tesler, M. (2016). *Post-Racial or Most-Racial?: Race and Politics in the Obama Era*. Chicago: University of Chicago Press.

Thompson, D. (2018, December 6). Millennials didn't kill the economy. The economy killed millennials. Retrieved June 18, 2019, from The Atlantic website: https://www .theatlantic.com/ideas/archive/2018/12/stop-blaming-millennials-killing-economy/577408/

Tribune Wire Reports. (2015, June 23). Obama says U.S. racism "not cured," makes point with epithet. Retrieved November 11, 2019, from Chicagotribune.com website: https://www.chicagotribune.com/nation-world/ct-president-obama-podcast-20150622-story.html

United States Department of Justice, Federal Bureau of Investigation. (2018). Hate crime statistics. Retrieved November 10, 2019, from https://www.justice.gov/hatecrimes/hate -crime-statistics

Vogels, E. (2019). Millennials stand out for their technology use, but older generations also embrace digital life. Retrieved November 10, 2019, from Pew Research Center website: https://www.pewresearch.org/fact-tank/2019/09/09/us-generations-technology-use/

Wodtke, G. T. (2016). Social Class and Income Inequality in the United States: Ownership, Authority, and Personal Income Distribution from 1980 to 2010. *American Journal of Soci-ology, 121*(5), 1375–1415. doi.org/10.1086/684273

Wolff, E. N. (2018). The Decline of African-American and Hispanic Wealth since the Great Recession (Working Paper No. 25198). doi.org/10.3386/w25198

Zucman, G. (2019). Global Wealth Inequality (Working Paper No. 25462). doi.org/10.3386/ w25462

Zukin, C., Keeter, S., Andolina, M., Jenkins, K., & Carpini, M. X. D. (2006). *A New Engage-ment?: Political Participation, Civic Life, and the Changing American Citizen*. Oxford University Press.

Conclusion

Black Millennials have a unique experience as they attempt to navigate the sociopolitical water that is life. The intersectionality of race and age is often challenged although the literature discussing these topics are few and far between. This collection of chapters hopes to open the door to examine ways in which Black Millennials navigate the world around them. By focusing on these key aspects of Black Millennials (racial identity, interpersonal relationships, employment, and social justice), the authors hope to start the conversation.

Having the authors themselves be Black Millennials allows for vulnerability to replace speculation. The authors are not just presenting data, they are presenting data infused with a lived-in experience that is both unique and collective. They are speaking to the part of the collective culture and giving a voice to those who may not have the same privilege. By doing this, the authors are allowing the narrative to change, which can begin the process of removing oppression.

This work highlights the importance of unlearning years of oppression by having individuals question their understanding of the Black Millennial experience. This is not the end but rather the beginning of giving individuals the opportunity to shape their learning by telling their stories. This can also be a tool to fight against the assumptions that other generations make about Black Millennials. Black Millennials are invested in doing the work to better themselves and their community. This book is evidence of that work.

Index

About the Editor and Contributors

Marisa G. Franco received her PhD and master's of science in counseling psychology at the University of Maryland. She received her bachelor's of science degree from New York University in applied psychology. She has published over twenty empirical articles on her research, which focuses on the health effects of racial identity invalidation—denying an individual's racial identity—for Multiracial individuals. She has also investigated the racial identity of mixed-race individuals, internationally, in Trinidad and Tobago, where she conducted a qualitative examination of the racial identity of Trinidadian douglas, who are of mixed race African/South Indian descent. Marisa has received numerous awards for her research and service including an award from the National Institute of Health, The University of Maryland A.L.L STAR Award, and the Ethnic Minority Achievement Award with commendations from the mayor of Maryland. She began a position as an assistant professor of counseling psychology at Georgia State University in the fall of 2017.

Neffer-Oduntunde Osunbunmi A. Kerr is a freelance writer and journalist who has written for *Ebony*, *Jet*, and other publications. Neffer was an in-house editorial contributor for the online magazine *On The DM* as well as one of the featured voices of the *Chicago Defender*. She has a blog called It's The Boom Show, which is featured on ChicagoNow, which is the official blog community for *The Chicago Tribune* publication. This writer is known for her blunt, transparent, and direct approach to politics, current events, and issues affecting her community. Neffer often employs humor in the form of satire and sarcasm to point out hypocrisy, societal double standards, and ideologies that are antiquated and out of date. The author does public speaking engagements, has facilitated workshops and seminars, and moderated panel discussions. As an independent consultant, she has worked closely with many Chicagoland nonprofits and arts organizations such as Muntu Dance Theatre of Chicago, The Beverly Arts Center, Betty Shabazz International Charter Schools, and others to develop impactful programs and projects within the community that focus on equity. Neffer is also a member of Zeta Phi Beta Sorority, Incorporated and serves on the South Shore Works, Arts and Culture Committee. She is currently pursuing her MBA with a concentration in project management.

Marcus D. Smith, LCPC, PhD, graduated from The Chicago School of Professional Psychology with a PhD in counseling education and supervision. He graduated from University of Maryland, College Park with a bachelor's in psychology in 2009, and a Master of Clinical Counseling from The Chicago School of Professional Psychology in 2011. His eight years of clinical and advocacy experience show a strong passion for working with underserved populations and families through a trauma-focused lens. Mr. Smith's advocacy also extends to his passion in writing. Currently Marcus is a contributing author to various works in academia. He's also a wellness blogger for MSmithfeedback, which partners with other professionals to discuss the unique experiences for people of color. Future writing opportunities certainly aim at providing education and insight to disenfranchised individuals on methods of healthy decision making. He's a dedicated advocate to marginalized communities and works diligently to ensure that all of his clients and readers of his written work are treated with the upmost compassion, respect, and care.

Natascha C. Dillon, PsyD, is a graduate of the American School of Professional Psychology (ASPP), Washington, DC campus's clinical psychology program. She also has a master's degree in counseling psychology from Bowie State University and a master's in clinical psychology from ASPP. Dr. Dillon has vast experience in conducting psychoeducational and psychological assessments, and treating children, adolescents, adults, and families with a variety of difficulties. Prior to obtaining her PsyD, she worked as a nurse in the areas of gerontology, mental health, youth detention, addictions, and with intellectually disabled populations. Although Dr. Dillon has been extensively trained in psychodynamic, cognitive/behavioral, Adlerian, family systems, and Gottman couples therapies, she utilizes an integrative approach tailored to meet the needs of her clients. Dr. Dillon currently provides individual, couples, family, and group therapy in the private practice setting in Charles and Montgomery Counties, Maryland. She has also conducted stress management seminars for the Miss Maryland Scholarship Organization and domestic violence workshops at the University of Maryland.

Vannesia Darby, MS, is an experienced, results-driven digital marketing consultant who has launched successful online campaigns for major brands such as Sony Music, Universal Music Group, and the YMCA. A dynamic public speaker and writer, she helps others pursue their passions while creating a vibrant culture of success. Her candid and thought-provoking blog posts have been published on online outlets such as *Teen Vogue, Blavity, Thought Catalog,* and *Madame Noire.* Owner of the digital marketing agency MOXIE Nashville, she strives to bridge innovation and motivation for her clients and workshop attendees. Committed to the empowerment of others, Vannesia holds a master's degree in management/organizational leadership from Middle Tennessee State University and a bachelor's degree in business management from Bradley University.

Leila E. Ellis-Nelson, PsyD graduated from The University of Toledo in 2009 with her bachelor's degree in psychology, her master's of clinical counseling (2012) and her doctorate in clinical psychology (2015) from the Chicago School of Professional Psychology. Her training was completed with a diverse clientele at Kennedy King College, Northwestern University, Bowling Green State University, Harper College, and Ada S. McKinley Behavioral Health Services. Some of her professional interests include the influence of societal norms on the ability of cultural minorities to obtain housing, mental health/physical treatment, further their career and higher education pursuits, and build healthier family dynamics. Her passion for these areas is evident in her work, volunteerism, and research; The Effects of Internalized Racism and Family Values on Higher Education Degree Attainment for African Americans [dissertation]. Presently, Dr. Ellis-Nelson is the associate director of Student Support Services at The Chicago School of Professional Psychology's online campus; co-owner of her private practice, Changing Perspectives; and cocreator of the multicultural counterspace, Coffee Hour Chicago, which serves as a free monthly opportunity for Black and Brown mental health and helping professionals to gather and work toward their professional and personal growth.

Candice C. Robinson, MA, is a PhD candidate in sociology at the University of Pittsburgh. Her dissertation uses a Black feminist lens to explore the relationship between the Black Middle Class, Civic Engagement, and Social Movements. Her case study of the National Urban League Young Professionals observes how participation in civic engagement over time by the Black Middle Class supports broader social justice aims. Candice has committed her career to conducting interdisciplinary scholarship that acknowledges the nuances of experiences of Black people in America.

Jacquelin Darby, PsyD, is a licensed clinical psychologist in both Maryland and Washington, DC. Dr. Darby received her PsyD from the American School of Professional Psychology's clinical psychology program. Dr. Darby completed her postdoctoral fellowship at American University Counseling Center and completed her APA-accredited internship at Howard University Counseling Services. Dr. Darby provides individual and group psychotherapy for young adults. Her clinical special interests include: substance use issues, body image concerns (specifically the effects of colorism), effects of systemic oppression on individuals, group therapy, and interpersonal trauma. Currently, Dr. Darby serves as a staff clinician at American University Counseling Center located in Washington, DC, and as staff psychologist at The Pinnacle Center located in Gaithersburg, Maryland.

www.ingramcontent.com/pod-product-compliance
Lightning Source LLC
Chambersburg PA
CBHW022326280326
41932CB00010B/1243